"What am I Going to do About You?" *he demanded.*

"Do I let you get into my blood?" He dropped his arm from the high fence to settle it against her shoulder, pausing only to flip his Stetson before claiming her waiting lips. The fire ignited between them as his arms became steel bands binding her willing body to his.

His fingers curled under her chin and he raised her face to question her soft, brown eyes.

She lowered her lashes so that he couldn't see the yearning there. "We'll have to wait and see what the future brings, won't we?" she whispered.

EDITH ST. GEORGE
is not only an accomplished writer but also a well-known landscape artist. The varied settings of her colorful fiction are as authentic and carefully drawn as her spirited characters.

Dear Reader:

Silhouette Romances is an exciting new publishing venture. We will be presenting the very finest writers of contemporary romantic fiction as well as outstanding new talent in this field. It is our hope that our stories, our heroes and our heroines will give you, the reader, all you want from romantic fiction.

Also, *you* play an important part in our future plans for Silhouette Romances. We welcome any suggestions or comments on our books and I invite you to write to us at the address below.

So, enjoy this book and all the wonderful romances from Silhouette. They're for *you!*

Karen Solem
Editor-in-Chief
Silhouette Books
P. O. Box 769
New York, N.Y. 10019

EDITH ST. GEORGE
West of the Moon

Silhouette *Romance*

Published by Silhouette Books New York

America's Publisher of Contemporary Romance

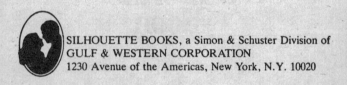

SILHOUETTE BOOKS, a Simon & Schuster Division of
GULF & WESTERN CORPORATION
1230 Avenue of the Americas, New York, N.Y. 10020

ISBN: 0-671-57069-2

First Silhouette printing March, 1981

10 9 8 7 6 5 4 3 2 1

America's Publisher of Contemporary Romance

Printed in the U.S.A.

Chapter One

Pins and needles pricked along her scalp. Debra glanced over her shoulder and tried to shake the feeling that eyes were following her progress into the shadowy glen. Bears had been reported in the area as well as moose, and both animals were known to have short tempers.

Raising her binoculars, she swept the field she had just left and then carefully examined the edge of the forest. She should have waited until another car came so she wouldn't be the only one taking this trail to Wraith Falls. It wasn't even indicated on the map given to everyone upon entering Yellowstone National Park, and most cars sped by the modest sign at the small parking area, thinking it only another rest stop.

Debra, however, was on the lookout for those signs after having been pleasantly surprised by little scenic gems. Perhaps most were deterred when they saw they had a half-mile walk ahead of them, but that had enhanced it for her.

The shade of the tall lodge pole pines was welcome and the bubbling brook danced before her. She paused, enjoying the refreshing coolness, then continued slowly along the path as it climbed alongside the stream cascading down the mountain. The noise increased and the promised waterfall came into view.

With a contented sigh she raised her camera and focused. When she returned to the city, she'd have one more picture to look at. Perhaps the colored print would help her recapture this peaceful interlude.

Reluctantly she rose, brushing at the pine needles clinging to her slacks. Time to go. There was a lot to see before her vacation was over.

"Wait," a deep voice commanded, and she gave a cry as she jumped in surprise. She swirled around, searching for its owner.

"Up here. On the cliff above you," he directed.

Debra squinted against the sun as she looked up. A khaki-clad figure sat leaning against the huge rock about fifty feet above her.

"Are you hurt?" she called in alarm. The precipice looked frighteningly perpendicular. "I'm not much of a climber, but if you direct me how to get up there, I'll see how I can help you."

"Go about two hundred feet further along the path. There's a ledge that leads up here."

Debra found the place. It was heart-stoppingly narrow but she made her way along it, wondering how she could possibly help the man down. He was still leaning against the rock, the usual hiker's knapsack next to him.

"I was searching for an unusual camera angle to take of the Falls and got myself out on a limb. I have a trick leg and it gave out," he said by way of explanation.

"What can I do?" she asked. One careless step and they both would tumble down.

He took a coil of rope and handed her an end. "I've been examining the trees. Pass the rope around that pine above me; I can tie one end around me and lower myself down. I was about to try my luck at tossing it up when I saw you coming."

Debra turned cautiously. He handed her the rope and directed her with barely suppressed impatience until she finally tossed it over the stout tree.

"I'll lower my pack first. When you untie it, I'll inch down."

Debra made the descent gingerly. She undid the knot and he tied the other end across his body. He swung over the edge and she held her breath as he dangled a moment in space. Using his good leg to keep himself from the wall of the cliff, he slid down in several pushes.

"You've done this before," she commented as she helped him untie the knots.

"Of course." He gave her a baleful look. It was self-evident.

For the first time Debra examined the man as he leaned against the stone wall. She was tall—five foot ten, but he stood over her by several inches. He was whipcord thin. Rays of sun shot through the branches, darkening deep shadows under the bony angles of his face, which had an overgrowth of beard. She then noticed the telltale paleness under his tan and the lines of pain along his mouth as he slowly lowered himself, carefully holding his left leg stiffly at an angle.

She started forward to assist him, then paused, realizing instinctively he would resent help.

He adjusted the angle of his leg and gave a sigh of relief before looking more closely at his rescuer. His blue eyes passed over her sable brown hair and her warm, brown eyes, then lingered an instant as they reached her wide, generous mouth. His glance dropped to her hands. No rings. Surprising for such an attractive girl. She looked about twenty-five. Surely, there must have been discerning men in her past. Not that it was his business, of course.

"Don't let me hold you. I have a stick strapped to the knapsack and can manage to make the road."

She sat down on the log she had occupied before. "I'm in no rush," she said quietly. "When you're ready, I'll walk out with you." Was it the pain making him this abrasive?

Settling his leg in a more comfortable position, he closed his eyes. The sparkle of perspiration on his brow caught her eye and she took a handkerchief from her pocket and dipped it in the cool stream. He looked up, startled, as she wiped his face.

"It's been a long time since anyone did that to me, he murmured, his blue eyes on hers.

She cocked her head to one side to examine him better. "I hope you don't mind. You looked as if a little refreshing coolness would help." She wished he wouldn't stare so intently at her with his electric blue eyes. They were very different from any she had seen. They were a clear light blue with a dark blue edging. The effect was piercing and disconcerting.

"Do you have anything left in that?" she asked, pointing to a thermos bottle protruding from a pocket of the knapsack.

They shared a cup of coffee in silence, then he inched his long frame up, leaning heavily against the boulder for support. Without a word, she shouldered his pack and stepped alongside of him.

"I'm a strong gal," she said. "Don't be afraid to lean on me if necessary."

He raised an eyebrow as he settled a battered Stetson on his head.

Deep brown eyes met clear blue ones. "You'd do the same for me if the role was reversed," she said briefly. He grasped his cane and limped forward.

The going was slow and he had to avail himself of her shoulder before they reached the parking area. Both were thankful to see the end of the trail. He was a big man, his rangy body masking his weight.

"Where's your car?" he asked when they rested before leaving the trail.

She pointed to the small motor van. "My home away from home. It belongs to a friend. We planned our vacation together. She got delayed and will join me in two days' time. She's seen Yellowstone already and we intend to go on from here, but where do you go now?"

"My truck is at the campgrounds at the Madison," he explained. "A neighbor was leaving this morning by the Northeast entrance and I talked him into dropping me off at Tower Falls. I planned to hike back, but you saw the end of that."

"Then I can take you back," Debra said, raising a

hand to halt his objection. "You'll have to hitch a ride there anyway so you may as well take my offer since I'm staying at the Madison also. I'm signed up for the next two days until I pick up Laurie. How long are you staying?"

"For another week. Like you, I have to work. Have to get back in time to drive the cattle down from the mountain to winter pasture before the snow comes."

Debra stared at him in delight. "How wonderful! I've been dying to meet an honest-to-goodness cowboy ever since I came west. Do you really work on a ranch with a horse and all?"

He managed to keep a straight face though laughter lurked in his eyes. "I really do, horse and all," he said solemnly.

"I noticed you wore a Stetson hat," she said. "But many men do even though they've never been on a ranch.

"I have read westerns ever since I was a teenager. I promised myself someday I would talk to a real live cowboy and find out what the West was really like," she continued. "That's one reason I moved from the East when my brother Dan was transferred to Denver."

"You keep house for him?" he asked.

"Oh, no. He's newly married. I have a minuscule two-room apartment that does nicely for now."

She unlocked the door to the van and adjusted the passenger seat to face the back. He managed the steep step up and sank gratefully into the comfortable seat.

He ran an appreciative glance over the compact

interior. Two tiered bunk beds were on one side with a bathroom and closet across from them. In front of him was the galley opposite the usual table and benches that could convert into another bed.

"This makes my truck look very primitive," he commented. "Wait until you see it!"

Debra glanced at her watch. "It's just time for lunch. How does a cup of coffee and a sandwich strike you?" she asked, opening a cabinet and handing him a towel. "You'll want to wash up after all that climbing," she said, pointing to the bathroom. "There should be enough hot water if you're careful."

The food was on the table when he came out.

"We haven't introduced ourselves," she said as he carefully inched into the bench seat. "I'm Debra Wayfield. Debbie to friends." She extended her hand.

"Marcus Reede, Marc to friends," he returned. He looked at her for a moment, then added, "Debbie is fine but I think you'll be Debra to me."

Debra blinked under the magnetic force of his gaze. There was something about this man. Her heart skipped a beat.

"Tell me about the ranch you work on. Is it large?" Talking would give her time to bring her breathing back to normal.

"Fairly," he said. "It has several hundred acres. Part of it is useless as range land though. It wraps halfway around a mountain. But the mountain streams formed by the snow water the land so that unless we have a series of unusually dry seasons, droughts seldom affect us."

11

"The owners picked well then," Debbie mused. "In a lot of the stories of the West, water was always a problem."

"Don't underestimate it," he agreed grimly. "I've seen ranchers go bankrupt when their wells went dry."

"Do you ride a horse all day?" she asked, her eyes dreamy. "I love riding and have so little opportunity."

"The jeep or truck takes us most places now, though horses are still necessary at times." he said matter-of-factly.

"Don't ruin my dream," she protested. "Modern ranching can't be that cruel. The cowboy always rode off into the sunset on a horse!"

He threw his head back in a burst of laughter. "You'll have to come visit the Double R," he said.

She leaned forward. "That would be heaven. To visit a real ranch, I mean," she breathed. "Do you think something like that could be arranged for just one day? They have garden tours in the East. Are there any tours of ranches out here? I bet Laurie would be thrilled also."

He took in her star-bright eyes. "It could be arranged if you want it. True Westerners are known for their hospitality."

She faltered before his offer. "It's nice to think about it, anyway," she said with an embarrassed laugh over exposing her innermost dreams so blatantly. She knew a ranch hand would have little to say about his boss opening his home to a stranger.

She rose, gathering the dishes. "We'll take off as

soon as these are done. I dare say you'll be happy to stretch out on your bed and rest your leg."

"I'll get over it quickly enough, he said briefly. "It was perfectly fine until I twisted wrong, shifting my weight on that narrow ledge."

"How did you injure your leg?"

"I came across a steer stuck in a gully. I roped and hauled it out. He ran a horn into my thigh in thanks."

She winced at the pain he must have gone through. The terse explanation left out the horror of the moment.

"I saw him coming and managed to escape with only a flesh wound. Luckily, I avoided an infection but the doctor ordered further rest so I decided I'd take a short vacation. I've never been to Yellowstone and I grabbed the opportunity to explore."

"I'm certain the doctor will be happy with your choice of a rest cure," she said dryly.

"I can't let the leg atrophy," he said with a shrug. "It's my form of physiotherapy. I have to get on that horse when I get back."

Debra frowned. "Won't your boss let you use the jeep until you heal completely?" she asked.

"He can be a hard taskmaster. Snow waits for no man and the cattle have to be brought down."

Had she detected a note of irony in his tone? "That doesn't sound consistent with your avowal he would offer his hospitality to me, she said. "I guess I will have to bury that hope. After all, I've had the dream of living on a ranch since I was a child. A mere visit of one day wouldn't be enough."

Wouldn't it, though! Any little stay would be relished.

They passed her alloted space in the campground and she drove him on to his truck.

"It looks as though I have a new neighbor," she said, pointing to her reserved spot. "I hope he is as congenial as the last one."

"I'm way at the other end," he directed. "No wonder I haven't seen you around. I'm stuck with a bunch of young college kids."

"Do I hear a tinge of derision?" she queried. "From what great age do you look down at them?"

He gave a rueful laugh. "At thirty, they seem very immature."

He could never be termed immature. She was well aware of the controlled vitality of the man beside her. He gave every evidence he met life head on and could take anything offered.

"And you?" he asked. "Or is it impolite to ask a young lady her age."

She shook her head. "I'll be twenty-five next month. My mother would have added—in a horrified whisper—'and on the edge of spinsterhood.'"

His glance slid over her. "If so, I'm sure it's by choice," he commented.

"Thank you, kind sir." She thought of Larry and Bill. It would have been so easy to accept their proposals. They were kind and gentle men but could only raise her temperature to lukewarm. Bill's persistence was one reason she decided to move west to follow her brother. Dan was her only living relative now.

Debra pulled up alongside the dusty half-truck. A

tarpaulin was stretched across the open back and lashed tightly to the sides.

"Don't you freeze at nights in a tent?" she asked, suppressing a shiver. These mornings a tentative edging of ice could be found on the puddles.

"I don't sleep in a tent," he corrected. He limped to the back of the truck and lowered the rear gate. "This is my home."

Debra looked in amazement at the mattress under the taut canvas. She glimpsed a metal locker and two large coolers as well as a Primus stove along one side of the truck.

He placed his backpack on the tailgate. "I'm quite snug in the sleeping bag. And the canvas keeps the elements at bay."

"Not bad," she said, admiring his ingenuity. "You have enough crawl space to maneuver. It's a lot drier and I bet a lot more comfortable than sleeping on the ground. How do you close the tailgate when you're in bed?"

"I don't bother," he admitted. "I prefer watching the stars. Of course, it has its drawbacks. I can't sit up in there. My living room is the cab. I have a lamp I can read by if I'm not ready for bed. It suits me fine but is too rustic to invite a girl to share."

"Oh, I don't know about that," she laughed. "I bet one of those young college girls you referred to so disparagingly would love the adventure."

Marc walked her back to her van. He held her hand before she entered. "I can't thank you enough, Debra Wayfield. I'm afraid I ruined one of your precious vacation days. When do you have to go back to work?"

"Actually, I have more than the two weeks we

planned," she admitted. "I'm a secretary to a lawyer. My boss is taking a month in Europe and his partner's gal Friday is holding down the fort."

His free hand went to her face as he brushed back a strand of hair blowing in the breeze. A finger lingered along her cheek and Debra found herself swallowing hard at the unexpected contact.

"Then you'll be able to spend more than one day at the Double R," he murmured.

Debra blinked in surprise. "Do you really think you can fix it with your boss?" she breathed.

"I'm certain," he said with conviction.

"Then I'll have to work it into our itinerary," she said, overwhelmed by a wash of incredible joy.

He glanced up at the lowering sun. "There's not much day left. What are you going to do now?"

"I'll go back to my spot. I've several letters to write as well as those 'having a wonderful time, wish you were here' cards."

He dropped his hands. "I'll see you later, Debra," he promised.

She nodded. So it was all set then.

The new neighbors were definitely not as nice as the last ones. Debra soon found out the three children were not enjoying the camping trip. They were too young to appreciate the grandeur of the scenery, and the harrassed parents were shooting daggers at each other.

Since the motor homes sat shoulder to shoulder, any voice raised in argument became community property. Debra slid the windows closed and turned the radio on low in a vain attempt at blotting out the whining cries from next door. The irritation rising in her precluded letter-writing so she concentrated on light notes on the cards.

When a strange man knocked on her trailer door, she was in no mood to act civil. She rose from the table with a sigh of irritation, wondering what he wanted to borrow.

Her annoyance was not camouflaged when she asked what he wanted. He was presentable enough. Gray slacks were a pleasant relief from the prevalent blue jeans, and the light blue polo shirt accented his eyes. His eyes!

She gave a gasp. "Marc!" she cried. "I didn't recognize you—you shaved!"

"That cool reception had me wondering if I made a mistake," he said wryly. He held out a paper bag. "I bring a thank-you offering. Two fillets from my freezer. I didn't know if you preferred them cooked under your broiler or burned over my Primus."

"That doesn't give me much choice, does it?" she laughed.

The sharp sound of a loud slap followed by a wailing sob came from the next trailer. The mother's strident voice rose above the child's cries.

Debra grimaced at the noise. "The new neighbors. They've been at it since I came. I just hope the children quiet down for the night.

"But come in, Marc. It's a little better with the door closed." She noticed he moved with less of a limp.

"You're walking better, I see," she said. "I was worried you'd push yourself."

"I indulged in a good nap, then treated myself to a hot shower and shave." He rubbed his hand along his smooth jaw.

She tilted her head as she eyed him critically. "I approve. It's a vast improvement, though a well-trimmed beard might be attractive also."

"My brother looks enough like me so you can decide when you meet him," he said.

"Does he work on the ranch also?" she asked.

"Yes," he answered slowly. At times his western drawl was very pronounced.

She was pulling the steaks out of the bag and didn't notice his hesitancy.

"Marc! They *are* fillets!" she exclaimed. "How in the world could you afford them!"

Again he hesitated as if choosing his words and she raised questioning eyes.

"The cook on the ranch packed one of my coolers with dry ice. Things have stayed frozen very nicely."

"Lucky us that she liked you enough to include such largess!" she said, impressed. "But then you have a surfeit of beef on a cattle ranch, don't you? Oh, Marc, I hope you can swing a visit for me without getting into trouble! I've been thinking of nothing else."

She swung the wide passenger seat so it faced the living quarters. "Anyone who can bring such luscious steaks gets the best seat in the house," she said. "Besides, it's too small a place for two to maneuver at the same time," she added.

The writing materials disappeared from the table to be replaced by gaily patterned mats. Baked potatoes and a fancy vegetable casserole came out of the small freezer and were put into the oven. The steaks were placed on the pan to finish defrosting.

"I wish I had wine to go with this," she said gaily. "And candles. I'm in a celebrating mood." A laugh died in her throat as she met his piercing blue eyes. A quiver ran through her and it took an effort to break the claim they put on her.

Careful, girl, careful, she warned herself. *This man has been around and won't be as easy to handle as past amours.*

"I'm afraid I can't help with the wine and candles, but perhaps a predinner drink?" Marc pulled out a flask from his hip pocket. "I hope you like bourbon."

"I've never tried it," she admitted, taking out ice cubes. "And a silver flask! I thought they went out with prohibition."

Marc grinned. "Some more stories you've read? This was Dad's. I carry it when working in cold weather. Sometimes it's the only way to get warm."

The meal was festive. The only annoyance was the intermittent wailing from next door.

"This friend, Laurie, who's flying in, is she also a secretary?" Marc asked.

"Yes. I met her since I moved here. We got along well from the moment we met. She's a little flighty, but fun to be with. This motor home belongs to her parents."

"I'm surprised your brother let you take off on your own." The disapproval in his voice made Debra look up. "You're too attractive a girl to travel alone."

Debra shook her head in exasperation. "You sound just like Dan. He didn't like the sudden change of plans either. Since Mom died, he thinks he must act as my guardian. Big brother is barely a year older and has to be put straight every now and then." Her smile was indulgent.

"Laurie was supposed to be with me but her boyfriend came back to town suddenly. It's been a torrid on-again, off-again affair. He wants to get married right away and she says she's not ready.

"Anyway, he called the morning we were to leave and said he was in town for a week. It caused a quick change of plans. I convinced her to do that and I'd go on. She's seen this park already so it gives me an opportunity to explore at my own pace. I'm to call tomorrow night and she'll tell me on what plane she's arriving the following day."

"Will she be willing to travel to the other side of Idaho?" he asked.

"She has no choice if that's where the Double R is," Debra said firmly. "She owes me that!"

Loud screams came from the next trailer. This time it was the husband and wife, and was only terminated when their door slammmed. Heavy boots grated on the gravel as the man stalked away. The children's cries took over, lifting into discordant shrieks.

Debra's face filled with distress. "Oh, the poor family. I hope they don't tear each other apart like that when they are home."

Marc's mouth firmed into an angry line. "This is no place for you," he said. He swung out of the door to return in a few minutes.

"I disconnected your electricity and hookups," he said. "Give me the keys to the van."

When her brother used that voice, Debra knew better than to argue. She complied while wondering what he was going to do.

He turned the van into the road and headed to his

end of the campground, then backed into an empty site next to his truck.

"At least you'll have peace here," he said grimly. "It's pretty late for anyone to claim this spot tonight.

"Don't look so worried," he said reassuringly, meeting her questioning gaze. "I'll straighten it out in the morning with the powers that be." He hooked up the outlets again before saying goodnight.

"The moon is gone," he said, looking up at the heavy clouds. "In fact a storm is brewing. Not afraid of lightning, are you?"

"No," she admitted. "In fact, I'm exhilarated by a good storm."

"This one will test your reactions," he said. "Have you ever been in a mountain thunderstorm? They can separate the men from the boys."

"Won't you get wet?" she asked. "Shall I put up your tailgate after you crawl under the tarp?"

"I'll pull down the canvas flap and hope it will do the trick. If not, I'll take to the cab."

"But you can't sleep sitting up, and your leg shouldn't be cramped like that," she protested.

The mocking eyebrow was again raised. "I'll manage." His cragged features softened slightly. A finger came up to push at the top of her nose. "Keep up like this and I might get to like being fussed over." His glance rested speculatively on her face. Then his mouth was on hers in a hard fast kiss.

He opened the door. "Lock this after me," he ordered brusquely.

He stepped out, then waited until she followed orders. He waved through the window before turning to his truck.

Her fingertips touched her pulsing lips while alarming trills ran along her nerves. She tore herself from where those thoughts were leading. After all, she barely knew this attractive stranger. She mustn't make too much of a casual good-night kiss.

Chapter Two

Thunder crashed overhead, reverberating angrily between the mountains, shaking the motor van in passing. Rain and wind slashed against the aluminum siding while lightning streaked the sky.

Debra sat up in the bed, hugging herself with excitement. Marc was right. This could separate the men from the boys.

Marc! The rain must be blowing straight into the open end of his truck. No flap of canvas could possibly keep him dry.

In one swift movement she was out of bed and groping in the closet for the weatherproof poncho.

The wind whipped rain into the van as she opened the door. She had to tug hard to close it. Lightning outlined a hooded figure similarly clad, struggling to close the tailgate. She helped slip the chain lock on the other side from him as the wind buffeted her against the truck.

Strong arms went roughly around her as he placed his body to take the worst of the wind and rain.

"What do you think you're doing, you crazy creature!" he yelled angrily above the noise of a crashing tree.

"I was afraid you were drowning." Debra screamed to be heard above the wind. "Come into my trailer where you can dry out."

He hesitated a second before leading her to the van. She had never been exposed to such a fierce display of warring elements, and was thankful for the protective arm around her. That last gust would have knocked her over.

"We better hang our ponchos here to drip in this step well by the door," she gasped when they finally made the protection of her motor home.

Even with the covering of the rain gear, she found her pajamas wet. She handed him a towel and they dried themselves as best they could.

"Heavens, are all your storms like this one?" she cried as another tree crashed to the ground.

"This is one of the better ones," he admitted as he toweled his hair. "It came on faster than I expected. The rain poured into my sleeping bag and I'm afraid my mattress is floating."

He narrowed his eyes while surveying her. The familiar flutter coursed through her.

"There was no need to go out into this storm and rescue me."

"Why not? I'd do it for a stranded cat, so why not you?" She attempted nonchalance. A shiver ran through her. It must have been the cold. And not because the most attractive man she had ever met was standing so close to her.

"Get out of those wet pajamas, woman, before you get pneumonia," he said in a hard voice. A muscle was jumping along his clenched jaw and something about his expression caused her to glance down.

Not until then did she see how the thin cotton material was molded damply to every soft curve of her body. Debra felt her cheeks flame as she turned hurriedly away. She fumbled in the drawer for a dry set and hurried to the bathroom.

"I'm afraid I don't have pants that will fit you," she called over her shoulder. He was clad in a damp sweater and denim slacks. "You'll find a bulky sweater in the closet that should stretch over your shoulders." She had been alarmingly aware how broad they were. "Also, you left your flask behind. A drink sounds appealing."

Debra came out shortly, wrapping a warm coat-sweater around her. Her nerves tightened when she saw the snug fit of her sweater across his wide shoulders. He was heating water on the stove and dividing the contents of the flask into two mugs.

The hot drink caused a welcomed warmth to course through her. They sat in the booth in the dark, sipping the hot whiskey and watching the lightning slowly recede. Thunder rumbled about their ears.

"It doesn't look as though the rain is stopping," she mused. "Do you think it will rain all night?"

"Probably," he said, putting down his empty mug. "I'd better dash across to my cab."

"No!" The word exploded before she could think. She took a deep breath to control her voice. "I mean, your leg wouldn't improve cramped on the seat. You're too tall to sleep there. I mean, there's no reason you can't take that upper bunk. It's past midnight and you need some sleep."

She hesitated as she saw his eyebrow raise.

"I—I mean, don't you think you should take the obvious solution?" Thank goodness he couldn't hear her pounding heart. Where did she get the nerve to voice such a proposition!

"I was thinking mainly of your injured leg," she concluded in a small voice.

Slowly his smile grew while listening to her stumbling. "You're thinking a lot of things, aren't you? Debra, you're priceless. A dry bed to stretch in is too much of a temptation to resist."

She looked at the upper bunk in question. "Can you climb up there?" she asked doubtfully. "You can use mine if it's easier."

The smile deepened into a mocking grin. "I've shared, but never put a woman out of her warm bed. If you feel modest, you better turn around while I undress."

She hurriedly complied, cheeks flaming. Soon she heard his satisfied sigh as he stretched out.

"Much more comfortable than the thin mattress in the truck," he admitted.

Debra hung his pants and sweater by the space heater. It was turned low against the cold but should dry his clothes by morning.

She shivered and pulled the blankets closer. She was all too conscious of his long length above her.

"Debra?" The deep voice floated down to her.

"Mmm?" she answered softly against the throbbing of her pulse.

"Thanks for rescuing me. Sweet dreams."

She gave a little sigh. "You, too, Marc."

Chapter Three

The sun's rays played across her face, awakening her. Debra stretched, giving a yawn before catching herself short. The mattress above moved and she remembered she had a roommate.

She recalled the torture, last night, of controlling her restless turning, too acutely aware of the man in the bunk overhead. It promised to be a sleepless night, then the hot drink mercifully did its job and her eyelids closed.

She slipped quietly out of bed and turned up the heater against the morning's sharp chill. His clothes had dried satisfactorily.

"Do you always run around so temptingly in your nightclothes when you have a male guest?"

Debra jerked around to see a tousled head lean over the side of the bunk. She decided to ignore his comment.

"I get first try at the bathroom, then you can have it while I fix you breakfast," she said. It was all more intimate than she was prepared for, and hoped she was carrying it off with the right amount of aplomb.

"You're spoiling me rotten,"

"Frankly, I'm buttering you up so you work hard at getting me to the Double R," she replied.

"Now hurry up and get ready for breakfast before I cast you out," she added. "You have work ahead of you, drying out your truck. Don't expect any more help from me!"

However, after cleaning the van, she relented. He had pulled the tarpaulin back and draped the damp mattress over the top of the cab. A very wet sleeping bag dripped from the tailgate.

"You should put this through the dryer," she said, wringing out the ends heavy with water.

He paused as he lifted down a metal camp locker. "You've got to be kidding. Can you imagine the condition of the people camping in tents? Several were blown over in that gale and they're lined up in the laundromat fighting for position."

Debra looked around, taking in the lines, draped with soggy clothes, hastily strung between trees.

She shook her head. "It looks like a refugee camp. Thank goodness the sun is out today and they can get reasonably dry before night. Do you think your bedding will be usable?"

He lowered himself from the truck and gave a shrug. "I've been damp before."

"I—I can lend you the blankets you used last night," she offered, lowering her eyes before his searching gaze.

"Thank goodness you're not including the bunk again," he said wryly. "There's just so much my blood pressure can take. I'm not used to having a sleeping beauty so near me. Next time I'd be dreaming myself into a prince and have to kiss her awake."

She gave him a startled glance. "I only act as a House of Refuge when the heavens open. Otherwise you're on your own. The offer of the blankets still holds though. Laurie's not due until tomorrow. If she comes."

Marc caught her doubt. "You're not certain?" he asked in surprise.

She shook her head with a sigh. "If her boyfriend stays longer, she may put off coming until he leaves or they have another fight."

"Sounds like a tempestuous affair," he said dryly.

"It is. The two fools are madly in love yet let their pride stand in the way of happiness."

"Would you?" he asked.

She raised eyebrows at him, not understanding his question.

"Let pride stand in the way of love," he finished.

A small frown creased her brow. "I don't know. I've never been in love. Yet I feel if I ever met the right man, I'd follow him wherever he led me."

Apparently he found these remarks not worth answering for he merely grunted as he lifted down the coolers and trunk. The wet floor of the truck was exposed now.

"I'll let you use my sponge mop," she laughed. "Let's see how efficient you are at housecleaning."

She brought out the mop and an additional large sponge. "You swing the mop and I'll see about drying off these boxes."

She went to work, humming contentedly. The sun glowed warmly on her back. She felt at peace with the world. Again, she squeezed the edges of his sleeping bag before adjusting it to get the full benefit of the sun. She opened his knapsack, angling it against the truck for the best flow of drying breezes.

Not until then did she look up to see how he was progressing. Marc was leaning on the mop handle, a quizzical expression on his face.

"Do you always sing while you work?" he asked.

"When it's a lovely day like this, yes," she replied, hoping her face didn't betray embarrassment.

"Hello, Marc. I see you've come off second best in the storm also."

Debra looked up in surprise to see a young girl saunter over. Her jeans were cut to the bare minimum, exposing smooth tanned legs. The tails of the unbuttoned cotton shirt were tied, baring the midriff as well as the deep cleavage.

She couldn't help glancing at the tall man beside her to see his reaction to all this exposure.

His eyes were all male as they swept appreciatively over the young girl. "Hello, Betty," he answered. "How did your group make out?"

She gave a shrug. "One tent blew over. They're sorting things out but I thought I'd see if you needed help."

His eyes became hooded. "I'm well taken care of. Thanks anyway." He turned to Debra. "Meet Betty—one of the college crowd I was telling you about."

Debra was reminded of his derogatory remark about the college kids appearing immature. This Betty was old the day she was born!

A sudden tightening invaded her chest. The girl was acting too assured with him to be just a passing acquaintance. Was she one who offered to share the inconveniences of his living quarters?

She shrugged against the unsettling sensation, happy when the girl moved on when Marc returned to work.

He removed his shirt before wrestling the mattress into another position. She became fascinated by the smooth play of muscles under the tanned skin and recalled the strong clasp of his arms the night before when the winds buffeted them. *Careful*, a voice whispered.

"After all your work, how about a cup of coffee?" she asked when he finished. "I'll warn you first, it's left over from breakfast."

He accepted gratefully. "It tasted fine the first time and can't be worse than what I make."

He opened the door and offered his hand to help her up the long first step into the van.

"Hi, Marc, see you're going in for a repeat, lucky fellow."

They both turned to meet the leering smile of a thin-faced man.

"Saw you bring her here last night and step out nice and dry this morning," he said, giving a knowing wink.

Debra's face paled, and she drew her breath in sharply at the expression on Marc's face. Never had she seen eyes turn so quickly to frozen chips of ice. The man backed away a step under their impact.

"Miss Wayfield was nice enough to offer a hot breakfast after a wet night. What did you do to help anyone?" he lashed out, his anger barely under control. The man gave a weak smile before turning to scuff away.

"I'm sorry, Debra," Marc said, his anger still showing. "I should never have let you be exposed to that." He turned to leave.

She placed a restraining hand on his arm. "Please, Marc, I still would like you to have that cup of coffee."

"No. You certainly can't think it wise after that!" His expression was forbiddingly remote.

The bite of tears hung behind her lids as she raised brown eyes to meet his gaze. She couldn't control the quiver to her lips.

"Don't let a small mind govern us," she begged in a low voice. "We have done nothing to hide."

His chest expanded sharply and he let out a long sigh. The slow smile gradually softened the taut lines on his face.

"Do you know your eyes can turn as soft as a doe's?" he said gently.

"You're just trying to flatter me into making fresh coffee," she said, glad the uncomfortable moment had passed.

"What are your plans for the rest of the day?" he asked as the coffee perked.

"I've seen all the scenic areas in the Park," she confessed. "I've seen Old Faithful erupt several times as well as some of the other geysers. I've been properly impressed by the bubbling mud and thermal springs. I've taken pictures of the moose gathering at dusk, and a herd of about forty buffalo plodding patiently in single file across a field.

"What I would like to do is go back once more to see the Firehole Canyon. The other day the rapids were deep in shadow. It was too late to take pictures."

He frowned. "The road in might be closed after the storm. There are a lot of loose stones on those cliffs."

"I'll chance it. It was so spectacular it's worth a second try."

"I'll drive you."

Debra couldn't hide her amusement. "I do believe you don't trust my driving. Your concern would please my brother."

"Your driving is fine," he said shortly. "It's the terrain I don't trust. It's easier to go along with you than worry about you."

"I remember some of the sharp curves, and also the sharp dropoff, so I'll gratefully accept your offer," she said. "It's almost noon. I'll make a quick sandwich for us to go with this coffee. Can you leave your truck open?"

"I'll ask someone to keep an eye on it. It would benefit from airing for the rest of the day."

Marc insisted upon driving the tortuous road. "Leave the driving to me," he said firmly. "You can't see the scenery properly and concentrate on this road at the same time."

The Firehole River was now a raging torrent, swollen by the night's heavy rain. Debra watched in awe when they parked in a turnoff.

"It was impressive before but now it takes my breath away," she cried, her voice raised to be heard over the muffled roar from the deep gorge. "The other day I thought it would be fun shooting those rapids in a rubber raft but I take it all back."

Marc was staring somberly into the deep ravine.

"If you owned a stretch like this would you want it opened to the public?"

Debra looked at him in surprise. Something in his stance warned her this was not a rhetorical question.

"It would depend on several factors," she replied slowly, sensing his deep perturbance. "Except for this road, this area has remained untouched. If it could be maintained as such, yes, I would be willing to share such beauty."

Why were the lines drawn so deeply around his mouth? Gone was the relaxed, easygoing person. An unknown, granite-hard man had taken over. She shivered at the thought of ever having to deal with him in this mood.

His eyes were cold as he withdrew to some remote area in his thoughts.

Debra glanced hesitatingly at him, then back to the deep canyon. She moved away, looking for the best spot to take a picture.

Steel fingers dug into her arm and she was jerked from the edge of the precipice. She was crushed against his hard body as he pulled her back to safety.

"You crazy woman, are you trying to kill yourself?" he grated.

Her senses whirled as she clung to him while trying to regain her balance. Then she was only conscious of the answering pounding of his heart against her breast.

"I—I was being careful," she stammered. "I was looking for a good angle to take of the rapids."

He released her slowly, shaking his head in exasperation. Then, picking up a stick, he moved to where she had stood. He jabbed hard at the flat rock she was about to step on. In horror she saw it slowly tilt and disappear over the side. A long pause later, a faint crash came up to them.

Debra's legs dissolved under her and she sank onto a rock. She raised a white face to Marc. He was instantly by her side. This time his arms were gentle around her as he cupped her head against his shoulder.

"We're a fine pair," he murmured, his voice rough with emotion. "We seem to be rescuing each other ever since we met. How did we manage beforehand?"

His hand ran soothingly along her silken hair until her trembling stopped.

His kiss was meant to reassure her. Instead her pulse leaped, leaving her curiously breathless. His eyes were coolly speculative as he took in the bewilderment displayed on her face.

"Give me your camera and I'll take those pictures," he said, releasing her. She longed to creep back into his arms, but instead handed him the camera clutched in her hand.

"How about making some coffee?" he said. "I think we both would enjoy a cup."

Debra nodded mutely and turned to the van with legs still shaking.

The mug of hot coffee felt good in her cold hands. She glanced apologetically at Marc as they sipped the liquid.

"I'm usually very careful. That rock looked quite safe," she said earnestly as he sat across from her in the booth.

"I shouldn't have been so rough but from my angle I could see how the rains had washed out the support underneath. I had to grab you fast." He leaned forward to run a finger over the bruise forming on her arm. "Did I do that?"

"I heal quickly," she reassured him, rising to place their cups in the sink. "One bruise is nothing to what might have been!"

Her eyes grew bright, remembering the horror of that long space in time before they heard the crash of the falling rock.

"Don't think about it, Debra!" He was beside her. His strong fingers curled under her chin, raising her pale face. He took in the still frightened expression, the dilated eyes, the tremor running along her generous mouth. His eyes lingered on the soft curve of her lips and his head slowly lowered until his mouth covered hers.

It started as before, a gentle kiss meant to reassure. Her hands crept up to his shoulders, clinging for support when he finally raised his head. There was no chill in his eyes now, but a questing need to evaluate her reaction. He saw the wonder in the brown depths and he gave a sigh as he gathered her close.

Debra had been kissed many times before but never like this. Never so she wanted to melt against a man in a glory of emotion. Never so her very soul cried for it to continue into eternity.

His muscular body was rock hard against hers, his arms steel bands that crushed her until it became difficult to breathe.

"Oh, Debra, Debra," he whispered with a half-laugh. "Forgive me. I could at least let you breathe!"

He cupped her face with his hands and placed butterfly kisses on the corners of her mouth. She could only stare dazedly at him as her pulse thundered through her body.

"You pack a wallop of a kiss, woman," he said, releasing her.

"I—I've never been kissed like that," she stammered, clinging to the side of the sink.

He jammed his hands in his pockets, his blue eyes sharp and speculative. "At this point I think I'd better go out and have a cigarette," he said abruptly.

He walked over to a tall pine and took the cigarette makings from his pocket as he leaned against the tree. Slowly the debilitating excitement melted into a controllable wonder. She went to the window and watched as he rolled the tobacco smoothly in the thin paper.

Debra turned to the sink to wash the mugs. For a man who had been merely a stranger who needed assistance twenty-four hours ago, Marc was occupying too much of her thoughts. It would be best for both of them if they returned to camp and to a natural parting of ways. Tomorrow when Laurie came they would take off on the rest of their planned vacation and she would see him no more.

She knew better than to expect anything from his promise of a visit to the ranch he worked. That was a farfetched dream. She winced against the tight feeling around her heart.

The talk was about the scenic wonders around them as he drove back to the campground. No mention was made of the kisses they shared, and she concluded that only she had been so decimated by their impact.

Her hands curled tightly in her lap. This response was what she had been seeking. The light pleasurable kisses shared with past boyfriends had left her vaguely restless, wondering if that was the height of emotion she was capable of feeling.

In a way she was sorry this cowboy had aroused her to such a degree. She would never be able to settle for less when it came time to choose a husband. Poor Bill had threatened to follow her. He didn't have a ghost of a chance after this.

Marc informed her he had already made her shift next to him official. "They said they had numerous complaints from other campers about your neighbors and gave them a warning."

"I have a sneaking suspicion the filler deep inside your bag is still damp," Debra said. "You better take my offer of blankets to use next to you."

A laugh glinted in his eyes. "Since you're not coming across with an offer for a repeat of the bunk, I'll make do with second best."

She turned to look at some people passing by so he wouldn't see her agitation. After that kiss there was no way she could spend a night with him in the close confines of the motor van.

"When are you going to call your friend?" he asked, changing the subject. He was astute enough to see how his teasing flustered her.

"Around six," she answered. "I hope she remembers to be home."

Laurie was there and Debra returned with a stunned expression on her face.

"Is something wrong?" Marc asked, seeing her disbelieving stare. "Can't Laurie make it?"

"No, and yes," she replied with a bemused laugh. "She's coming all right. With her husband. She and Dick were married by special license and they want me to get them a room at one of the inns here to continue their honeymoon."

"You don't look very happy for them," he said, studying her face.

"Oh, I am. I'm being selfish about myself. It just hit me there goes the rest of my vacation. This motor home belongs to her family so I have no choice but to give it to them." A sigh slipped out. "I better call the airport and see if they have a seat back to Denver. There goes my hope of visiting a real working ranch. That's what I get for building on a dream." She gave Marc a rueful smile.

"Don't decide anything this second, Debra," he ordered. "Let's talk over a cup of coffee."

He brought in a sponge cake. "My contribution to go with the coffee, compliments of Aunt Elsie. Also two more steaks if you can face having them two days in a row!"

"Now you're being facetious! Is Aunt Elsie the cook at the ranch?"

"Ah—yes," he said, concentrating on cutting thick slabs of the cake. "She knows this is my favorite cake."

"Mm, delicious!" Debra agreed after taking a bite. "I love baking! Too bad I won't see her to ask for this recipe."

"Why won't you?" he asked. "There's no reason to give up your visit to the Double R. You could come with me after handing over this van to Laurie and her new husband."

He held up a hand to stop her involuntary protest. "Wait to hear me out. We'll both drive to Yellowstone Airport tomorrow, and after transferring your things to my truck you can wish the honeymooners bon voyage and take off with me. We can make the ranch in two days."

Debra was speechless as she took in his suggestion. To see ranch country and not have to go back to the confines of the city right away! The dream bubbled along then burst as she faced reality.

"Thanks for the offer, Marc, but everything is different now. Before, I would be with a girlfriend and have a private van to stay in. Now I would have to be put up for the night and you can't expect your boss to be happy with that situation thrust upon him."

Her eyes grew large as she leaned forward in dismay. "Or are you putting me in the bunkhouse with the cowboys?"

"No, Debra, I'm certain you would be treated as an honored guest." His eyes were mocking.

She couldn't contain her doubts. "I don't understand. Are you a relative? I mean, why should the owner of a ranch as large as this Double R appears to be feel obligated to offer his hospitality to someone his ranch hand brings back with him?"

"I repeat. You will be an honored guest. You will have to trust me or forget about the whole thing. You'll understand when you get there."

Should she trust this handsome stranger? She had known him such a short time! But then, a voice urged, never again would she have such an opportunity to have her dearest dream come true.

She stared into his blue eyes, then the corners of her wide friendly mouth turned up in a slow smile. "Zane Grey wins," she capitulated. "His books were my constant companions as I grew up in New York City. My dreams were built of the wide-open spaces he so lovingly described. I'd never forgive myself if I didn't selfishly grab at this opportunity you offer."

"Thank you for your trust, Debra," he said briskly. "I know just the horse for you. You'll get all the riding you want."

She gave an excited laugh. "I haven't been on a horse in ages. I hope he's gentle!"

"He is. Jacko is one of the first horses I broke in and is a very settled old man now. We'll start with him until you build a few protective calluses."

"Marc, I'm not following you!" Her voice was startled. "I thought I was only staying overnight!"

His lids dropped, shuttering the piercing blue of his eyes. "You said you didn't have to return immediately to work. A week would barely be time enough to show you around. You don't want to miss seeing the whole setup, do you?"

She looked at him, enthralled with the thought. A week!

All through dinner Debra tried to get a more complete picture of the personnel and especially of the owners of the ranch. She had learned nothing about them except there was an Aunt Elsie in charge of cooking.

Marc did not enlighten her, preferring to talk about the ranch. With October around the corner, they would soon be bringing the cattle down from the higher ranges. There was a new quality in his voice as he talked. Debra recognized his enthusiasm for his way of life. She could now understand why, though he seemed well educated, he was content to be a ranch hand. Who could blame him for doing what he loved? Too many men were faced with dreary lives making a comfortable living but hating the work that paid their bills.

"If you feel brave, you might try a trip to the top corral," he continued. "The calves are branded there before taken to the winter pasture."

She could have listened to him talk into the night. It was dark outside when he halted, giving a low chuckle.

"You keep listening with those stars in your eyes, Debra, and you'll never be able to shut me up. We'll be here until the small hours. There's nothing like an appreciative audience to keep me spouting on my favorite subject."

"I can see ranching is in your blood," she murmured. "It wouldn't take much for me to scream for Equal Rights in capital letters and demand a chance at being a ranch hand!"

He receded behind a cooly speculative appraisal. "Most women can't take the life. What makes you think you can? You've been softened by city living. There's no store around the corner. There's not even a movie in our town, and the mountains block out television.

"But most wives live for their husband and his happiness," she asserted unaccountably angry.

"You *are* a romantic!" he mocked.

"Then good luck to you when you plan to make the plunge!" Debbie was proud she was able to keep her voice light. There must be many girls vying for this striking man. How had he remained a bachelor so long? Something drove her to ask.

"Surely in your thirty years you must have found some girl who more than appealed to you?"

His jaw tightened. "One or two, but something always came up to cool the fires. And you?"

"A few. But I felt there was something missing and it made me draw back before committing myself." How could she explain her reluctance to settle for what seemed less than best?

There was a moment of silence. Then Marc rose from the table. "It's getting late, and I feel the need for bed. Last night's storm cut into my sleep. And don't forget, you'll have to pack your things if we have to be at the airport by nine."

He departed with the two blankets from the bunk and she forced herself to concentrate on gathering her belongings.

She had no suitcase since she had brought the van to the door of her apartment to transfer her clothes. She ended by packing as neatly as possible into large plastic bags. She would not make much of an impression on Marc's employers. Perhaps she could sneak them into her room one at a time.

She met Marc as she came from the showers. The sun had not crept over the mountains long enough to warm the morning air, and she shivered as she greeted him.

"Breakfast in half an hour if it's all right with you," she called. "I packed and scrubbed everything last night. The sheets and towels are in the dryer already and as soon as they're done I'll make up the bunks so everything will be ready for the honeymooners."

He brought the blankets with him and also a large paper bag.

"A gift for the newlyweds," he said. "I didn't see any reason to return with the rest of this meat. There are some more steaks as well as lamb chops which I'm sure they can use."

"Laurie will bless you." she cried. "I feel better now because I won't have time to fill the refrigerator for them. This will be a real wedding present.

They arrived at the airport just in time to see the small silver plane circle for landing.

Debra couldn't hide her nervousness. Now that her clothes were packed in the back of Marc's truck, she was having second thoughts. She wondered how to explain to Laurie this jaunt across the state with a comparative stranger.

Laurie flew to Debra, her happiness bubbling over as she hugged her friend.

Any apprehension that Laurie would question her decision soon dissipated. The new bride and groom were too happy to find the motor home was theirs for their honeymoon to worry about her switch of plans. Besides, Dick took an instant liking to Marc and his approval was enough for Laurie. When they saw the freezer filled with the succulent meat, Laurie went into raptures.

"I'm relieved you don't want the van anymore," Laurie confessed as they had a final cup of coffee. "Mom and Dad said we could take it to Dallas and use it until we found a decent place to live. They'd then fly down to see us and drive it back."

"As soon as I have an address, I'll write," she promised. "I expect to hear all about your adventure, you lucky girl.

"And, Marc, I hope you don't cause Debbie's dreams to come tumbling down. Every clear day she stares at the mountains and vows she'll get to see some ranch even if she has to sneak down a private road and pretend she innocently followed the wrong turnoff!"

Then with a final hug, she whispered in her friend's ear. "And if you let that hunk of man get away, I'll never speak to you again, Debbie Wayfield!"

The sky was a vibrant blue with not a cloud in view. Debra settled in the truck next to Marc.

"At last!" she said with a sigh of bliss. "I could giggle like a schoolgirl from excitement."

"Debra, you look like a sixteen-year-old going on her first date! I'm not going to be able to satisfy your dream completely, you know. Reality is never the same. But I can give you views that will take your breath away, and a chance to see how a big spread works."

He leaned forward to insert the ignition key. "This is it, Debra. Your last chance to escape."

She looked at him, startled. He was staring ahead. His jaw was clamped tight and a muscle twitched along the edge.

"What an odd thing to say," she said, suddenly uneasy.

He turned to meet her bewildered gaze and his eyes became hooded. "The roads we'll be traveling are pretty isolated and will give you no opportunity to change your mind."

"You mean we'll be finally in the wide-open spaces?" she said, not convinced that was what he had meant. He nodded slowly.

"Good. It's what I've been looking for. What are you waiting for, driver? We've got tracks to make! How's that for cowboy lingo!"

His glance was evaluating. "Not bad," he said.

"I've a feeling this trip back is going to be more interesting than I had anticipated."

He pulled off the road at noon and Debra made sandwiches while he worked the stove to perk coffee and heat a can of soup.

They sat in the shade of the truck. The sun was warm now, taking the chill off the morning.

"Is that stream safe to wash these?" she asked as she gathered the dishes.

"It will be cold, but you won't find it contaminated," he promised.

She observed his amused expression when she returned. "Something strike you as funny?" she queried, shivering as she tried to rub warmth into frozen fingers.

"You don't look city born and bred now. I've taken country girls out who would be insulted to sit by a roadside for lunch and then clean up in a mountain stream."

"That's their loss." She grimaced, blowing on her bright red fingers.

"I warned you these streams guarantee to freeze." He came over to take her hands in his warm, large ones.

This position was much too intimate. He was inches away and she submitted to his scrutiny. Her gaze dropped to his chest. The tab of his tobacco pouch hung from his pocket and she grabbed at the safe subject.

"I was fascinated yesterday when I saw you roll a cigarette. When Dan and I were young we tried it. She laughingly described the disastrous results.

"It discouraged us enough so we didn't try to smoke again for a couple of years. Our poor parents.

I don't know how they survived raising us. Dan is a year older and what he didn't think up, I did. That was the period we decided to buy a ranch when we grew up and live happily ever after."

She prattled on, knowing she was babbling foolishly, but was unable to stop. Anything was better than letting this lightheaded sensation swamp her. "If it isn't difficult to learn, would you teach me how to roll one? I can just see Dan's face when I return home and give a demonstration!"

"I'll give you the first lesson," he said. "No, leave your hands in mine a little longer," he commanded as she started to pull away.

He showed her how he placed his finger to bend the paper, the precise amount of tobacco, and the quick roll and lick to the paper to seal it. The resulting cigarette was perfectly formed. Their heads touched as she watched the procedure.

"It looks so easy," she sighed. "I'm afraid it will take more than a week to learn."

"No reason why it should. I learned in an hour," he said. "You try now and I'll direct."

Even with his hands cupped around hers directing the movements, the result was a sorry imitation. The contact was turning her usual dexterous fingers into thumbs.

"We'd better stop or you won't have the makings for any more," she laughed, thankful to be able to step away from his intoxicating presence.

"Shall I make you one?" he asked. "I haven't seen you smoke."

"I usually don't," she admitted. "Sometime I would like to try one to see how it tastes."

He lit his cigarette and handed it to her. "The

flavor is different from commercial brands," he warned her.

She inhaled, well aware his lips had been there first. "More full-bodied," she pronounced, handing it back. She hoped she sounded sophisticated.

They repacked the truck and she moved to the cab, eager to get to the ranch. She was stopped, pinned to its side, his hands braced on each side of her.

"We forgot something," he said. When she looked at him questioningly, he added, "Dessert time."

She stiffened. She didn't know if she liked what his kisses were doing to her. In a few days' time he would be a memory she had to forget.

"No . . . please," she whispered.

An eyebrow flicked upward as his face came closer. The blue eyes were bright mirrors, showing nothing.

They were not touching except for their mouths, and there they became welded together.

She leaned weakly against the truck when he lifted his head. There was a sharpness in his gaze now. He turned silently and opened the door for her, and she climbed into the cab.

Debra was forced to take several deep breaths in an attempt to control the tremors running through her, and finally resorted to scolding herself.

What in the world was the matter with her? She had been kissed many times before. It must be that excitement of attaining her dream to finally be on a ranch was flowing over, she conceded, adding enchantment to a cowboy's kisses. Perhaps if he weren't so handsome . . .

Determined Marc would not see her susceptibility to his kisses, she searched for a safe subject to pursue.

"We have to stop at the next town so I can buy a pouch of tobacco. I promise not to practice in the truck." Suddenly her sense of humor came to her rescue. Her eyes danced, envisioning the chaos of the next few attempts at rolling a cigarette. "Promise you won't laugh at me, Marc!"

"Not a twitch of the lips," he promised solemnly. The trail of smoke across his face effectively hid the deepening laugh lines.

Debra settled more comfortably in the seat. Her composure now restored.

"What type cattle do they run on the Double R?" she asked. She had discovered the first day that he could talk for hours about the ranch.

"Principally Herefords," he said, his face already lit with enthusiasm. "We do have some Angus also but they're ready to be shipped to market."

Debra recalled the delicious steaks he had brought to the van for their enjoyment, and the price they rated at the meat counters. Her eyes widened as she began to understand something of the amount of money each animal represented.

"Ranching must be a very profitable business," she said in awe.

"It's a decent living now," he admitted. "But there were many lean years when ranches folded." He darted a swift glance at her. "Don't think that we get anything close to what you have to pay at the market. There are too many middle men who need their slice of the profits. True, the rancher is getting more than he used to, but the cost of hay, grain, everything, has skyrocketed. Plus the ranch hands naturally need a decent increase also."

Debra was silent, digesting the information. When bemoaning the rising cost of that pound of hamburger, she never realized the many reasons why.

"Is it a large ranch?" She was trying to envision the place. She had heard of a spread in Texas that was hundreds of thousands of acres.

"Large enough," he said. "It takes in a mountain and then some."

She looked at him in surprise, recalling the rolling plains mentioned in the novels she read. She looked doubtfully at the somewhat precipitous sides of the mountains they were passing, and wondered how cattle could find footing to navigate them, far less search for grass to survive. The sagebrush was everywhere, the bane of cattlemen.

As usual, he seemed sensitive to her thoughts, a habit that was becoming disconcertaining. His hand went out and squeezed hers reassuringly.

"Don't look so confused. Wait until you see the set-up and you'll understand. Our mountain is unique but you have to see it to know what I'm talking about.

"You'll notice as we go along that these mountains are two-faced. The winds carrying rainclouds are from the west and are frequently too heavy to lift over the tops. As a result the rainfall is heaviest on the western flank. Notice how the west sides are consistently greener, with a heavier growth of trees while the east side looks quite barren.

"Our mountain is the same." His lips tightened as

if in bitterness before he continued. "Unfortunately, our west side is too precipitous to make grazing feasible. It does, however, have great catchment basins and the runoff streams help irrigate the eastern slopes. That's where we have our pastures."

Debra tried to picture what he was describing but decided to wait until she saw it. His explanation would then be clearer.

A new excitement invaded her. Soon, very soon, she would enter the working world of the rancher, would even be riding a horse, perhaps observe a round-up. She looked at the cowboy who was making it all possible, and was filled with a glowing happiness.

"Marc," she said softly, "I want to thank you for finding a way to get me to your ranch. I don't know how to show my appreciation."

He glanced at her, an enigmatic smile on his lips. "We'll just have to think about that, won't we," he replied just as softly.

A thought suddenly struck her and she glanced warily at him. "You said it takes two days to reach the Double R," she said. "How far do you plan to go today, and don't you think we should have called ahead for reservations?"

He glanced at her. Upon seeing her perturbed expression, the creases at the corner of his eyes deepened as if in silent laughter. "I thought we'd take pot-luck," he said casually.

A tiny frown started between her brows as she stared at her hands clasped tightly on her lap. What did he mean? Was he thinking those few shared kisses could lead to something more—like a shared motel room? Her heart beat heavily in her chest as she considered her situation. She knew nothing about this cowboy whom she had so blithely decided to accompany. Her crazy dream to see a ranch had blinded her to what, under cold rational evaluation, was an extremely foolhardy excursion.

The corners of his mouth twitched a second before he returned his attention to the road. "We'll be staying at a friend's ranch," he said finally. "You said you liked to examine them closer and I thought you'd be interested in his since it is different from the Double R. You see, he raises horses."

Debra couldn't prevent the sigh of relief escaping and Marc rubbed his hand over his mouth before he looked at her again.

"Doesn't it appeal to you, Debra?" he asked with mock concern. "We can forget about it and find a motel for the night if you so prefer."

"Oh, no!" she protested quickly. Then, seeing the glint of amusement in his eyes, she became overwhelmed with confusion. Had her face displayed her concern? Her brother had often berated her when they were children for revealing their mischievous acts to their parents by her guilty expression.

She stared stiffly ahead, lips compressed, furious that he was aware of the cause of her embarrassment. In comparison to his poised self-assurance, she must appear childishly immature. The realization was dismayingly deflating.

They rode several minutes in heavy silence before Marc pulled the truck to the verge of the road. He pointed to the field beside them and Debra gave a gasp of pleasure. A small herd of pronghorn antelope were grazing short yards from them. They appeared delightfully small and dainty in comparison to the deer she was used to in the east.

"Oh, Marc, how absolutely darling!" she enthused. She watched, entranced, as two youngsters butted each other in imitation battle. The buck stood to one side, proudly aloof, an alert sentinel over his harem. He stiffened suddenly, giving an alarm. There were flashes of white and instantly the herd disappeared.

Laughing in delight, she turned to Marc, wondering if he had enjoyed the little exhibition as much as she had. She found his gaze on her and realized he had been intently examining her.

A faint flush tinted her cheeks. He ran the back of a finger over its silken outline, a bemused smile softening his firm mouth.

"You constantly amaze me, Debra," he said softly. "Sophisticated and assured one minute, and the next an entrancing child. I shall enjoy showing you about the ranch to watch your reaction. We have many lovely sights for you to see."

He watched the blush deepen with increased amusement before leaning forward to turn the key in the ignition. It wasn't until several miles had passed that Debra realized the uncomfortable atmosphere in the cab had passed, and that he had deliberately stopped to show her the antelopes with that result in mind.

This cowboy, this too-interesting man, was proving remarkably understanding, and a warmth flowed through her. She leaned forward with heightened expectation. Suddenly she was anxious for the ride to end and this unforeseen adventure to unravel.

The high mountains were casting purple shadows on their western slopes when he turned under a swinging sign hanging from tall gate posts.

"Lazy K-A." she read. "Is this your friend's ranch? I hope you called to warn them I was along!"

He glanced across his shoulder at her. "You have a lot to learn about western hospitality, Debra. It's a two mile run into their homestead and they'll see the dust from our truck long before we get there. That's enough warning. They'd be insulted if they found I drove past at supper time and didn't drop in. And to spend the night at a motel would be unforgivable. I would feel the same way."

She wished she could wash some of the dust away and change to something besides faded blue jeans. It was suddenly important to make a good impression on his friends. She reached surreptitiously into her pocketbook for a lipstick and mirror.

"These potholes should produce an interesting result," he said before slowing the truck to a stop. He had seen what she was up to after all. "Are you insisting on a full make-up job?"

"Only a little lipstick," she confessed. "My clothes are a mess so you'll have to forgive my little vanity. I'll let you in on a secret. It's woman's age-old way to raise some confidence."

He smiled while watching critically as she applied the coloring and combed her hair. "With your lovely skin you don't need artificial covering," he said with approval. "Nothing is more disconcerting to me than a woman in full war paint. I keep wondering what she is hiding."

"Nothing, I'm sure," she said with a laugh. "It's a habit to some."

"Then promise me one thing, Debra. Don't succomb. I like the touch of the smooth texture of your skin. It would be a crime to cover it."

"Even under all this dust?" She gave a light laugh to hide the flutter in her breast.

He ran his knuckles over the grit on his cheek. "A shower will feel good," he admitted.

"What are your friends' names?" she asked as he started the truck again.

"Kenneth and Abby Mackel," he answered. "Hence the brand—Lazy K-A. I went through college with Ken and we've remained good friends. He married Abby two years ago and I believe they're expecting shortly."

A tall, dark haired girl was waiting on the wide porch stretched across the front of the house. Her face broke into a welcoming smile when she recognized the driver.

"I don't believe it! How wonderful to see you, Marc! This will make Ken's day. He just came in and is unsaddling his horse." She came down the steps with outstretched hands, her face raised for his kiss.

"You're pretty as ever, Abby, in spite of the expansion," he teased. Placing an arm across her shoulder, he drew her to the side of the truck.

"Abby, meet Debra Wayfield. She's traveling with me to the Double R."

The woman barely managed to hide the quick flash of surprise as she reached for Debra's hands. "Welcome to the Lazy K-A. How wonderful to have another woman at supper! Maybe the ranch talk will be a little diluted, though that's faint hope!

"Go and hunt up Ken, Marc," she ordered. "If

56

he didn't see your dust trail he'll find a hundred and one things to do before reaching the house."

Relief flooded Debra as Abby urged her to the house. Marc was right. Abby couldn't act friendlier. Already she felt like an old family friend.

"You're staying for supper, of course," Abby chatted happily as they went into the large comfortable living room. "And since you can't make the Double R before tomorrow afternoon, you'll have to stay overnight."

"Marc mentioned it," Debra confessed, still feeling embarrassed over his assumption she would also be welcomed. But the girl's obvious delight over having them was reassuring.

"You'll be wanting a shower before we eat. Aren't the roads awfully dusty! It's either that or muddy quagmires," Abby said with resignation. "You'll have plenty of time if I know those two men. They'll eventually remember we're here, or more likely their appetites will tell them, and will need to clean up, so take your time."

The shower felt heaven sent. Debra wished there was time to shampoo her hair but settled for a thorough brushing. She would dearly love to dress up for Marc but in consideration of the enlarged figure of her hostess, decided to forego any glamour.

Instead, she put on black slacks and a red silk blouse that had a long fringed sash. She swirled her hair into a chignon on top of her head and teased a soft ringlet over each ear.

Minimum make-up, she warned herself. Marc had been firm about that. The lipstick matched the scarlet of her blouse and she added a final spray of perfume.

She had been hearing the male voices and the shower running so she knew the men had arrived. Perhaps she could help Abby with the extra work their arrival was giving her, she thought, and went to the kitchen.

Abby greeted her cheerfully. "I could kill you. You're much too pretty. I could do without your competition," she said, gazing despairingly at her figure.

"Don't say that!" Debra said quickly. "I'm sure, as far as your husband is concerned, no one can compare with you."

"Thanks, for the kind words," she said with a laugh; then, looking over Debra's shoulder, added, "You heard the girl. What's your comment?"

Debra turned to see Marc standing in the doorway. He must have entered right behind her.

His eyes traveled lingeringly over her. "I can't speak as a husband, but as a man I'd say you're both right. I'd be proud to have a wife like you, Abby, and yes, I think this gal can be classed as pretty."

"It's a case of clothes making the woman," Debra said lightly. "Anything is an improvement after those old jeans I've been wearing."

"Perhaps," he said, and as his light blue eyes pierced hers, she knew he was thinking of another night when damp nightclothes had clung to her body and he had ordered her brusquely to change.

"So this is Debbie!" The voice boomed into her musings.

Ken was slightly shorter than his friend, but he emanated the same vibrant force. That he was also very much in love was evident, for after shaking her hand in greeting, he strode to his wife and kissed her tenderly.

"Everything okay, honey?" he asked.

She nodded as her hand went to his face in a caress, and for a moment in time they were alone in their private world.

"Marc tells me he's in your debt for rescuing him when his leg gave out," he said while mixing cocktails after they settled in the living room.

"It wasn't that dramatic," Debra smiled. "But I'm happy he thinks so. In payment he's taking me to see the Double R. I've been dreaming a long time about seeing a working ranch. I only hope his boss is as agreeable as he promises. I'd hate to create a problem."

Ken's drink stopped in mid-air and Debbie caught the surprised glance he shot at Marc sitting beside her on the sofa.

A shiver of apprehension swept her. Was Marc being over-optimistic about his employer receiving a visitor? She hoped she wouldn't cause him trouble. To hide her concern, she turned to Abby.

"Marc has been warning me about the hard life ranching is to a woman. Do you find it so?"

"I guess it could be so labeled," she answered. "But it has its moments. In fact I wouldn't want any other life." Her eyes rested tenderly on her husband for a second. "There's nothing glamourous about it, I assure you. It's pure unadulterated work when needed to help with rounding up strays at branding time and the thousand and one things that constantly crop up. But when you go to bed you can't help being satisfied."

Ken smirked as he cleared his throat, and she laughingly threw a pillow at him.

"Debra assures me she can ride," Marc said. "I plan to take her to the top corral so she can see what I mean."

"I hope you'll be easier on the poor girl than Ken was with me," Abby cried. "When he first introduced me to the ranch before we were married, he was so eager to show me everything, he rode me to pieces. I couldn't move for two days!"

"I've warned Marc I haven't done much riding lately and he promises to give me a sedate mount."

The talk went naturally to the latest lot of horses Ken had just bought.

"If you need some good quarter horses, I've got a few extra," he told Marc. "And before you leave tomorrow, you have to see an interesting filly I got at a bargain. She needs some gentling. I thought Abby would like her but she won't part with her old faithful."

"I'm being practical, love," she protested. "My riding days will be curtailed with Junior taking up my time. It wouldn't be fair to have that new beauty stay idle."

Seeing her interest, Ken promised Debra a look at the horses before they left in the morning and she went to bed with pleasant anticipation.

The following morning the sun woke Debra all too soon. She hurried into old denims. Finding the house quiet, she tiptoed through it to get her quilted jacket she had left in the truck. It was a necessity with the sharp bite in the morning's air.

"Up already?" Marc called. The two men were

coming from the stable looking as if they had already put in a few hours work.

Debra's face fell in disappointment. "Oh dear, am I too late? You didn't give me a time to get up, and I so wanted to see the horses!"

"We haven't been to the paddock," Marc assured her. "We were helping a lazy foal see the light of day."

"A new baby!" she exclaimed. "Oh, Marc, why didn't you call me! I would have loved to see it. I might have been able to assist you."

"That would be reaching a new high," Ken laughed. "Two vets and a nurse could have scared old Sally into behaving better."

Debra's eyes grew large with amazement. "You're a veterinarian?" she questioned Marc accusingly.

"A veterinarian and a cowboy," he admitted, his eyes glinting while watching her reaction to the startling news.

"Let's get some breakfast," Ken said, unaware of her consternation. "Then we'll let you see the new foal—baby!" he exploded, rolling his eyes skyward while suppressing a grin.

Ken's revelation about Marc's profession filled Debra with elation. She admitted becoming suspicious about Marc's position at the Double R. It didn't seem feasible an ordinary cowboy could be so positive she would be welcomed there. But a veterinarian held an important position on a ranch. It must be a large spread to afford his personal services.

The picture was in better focus. He had impressed her as being well educated. There was an aggressive assurance in his carriage that she doubted a mere cowboy would possess.

Abby was busy in the kitchen and Debra hurried to help her. Her astonishment grew upon seeing the enormous breakfast being prepared. Besides halved grapefruit and hot cereal, there were eggs and lamb chops, hot cornbread and endless cups of coffee.

The men ate with relish, leaving her to marvel at how they could still retain such lean, muscular figures. She was beginning to appreciate the hard work involved in ranching which kept them honed down, sinew hard, in spite of the calories ingested.

Abby apologized to Marc over his interrupted sleep. "We don't usually expect guests to pay for their supper!" she exclaimed.

Marc smiled reassuringly. "Don't fret, Abby. I enjoyed the opportunity to be with Ken. It was like old times. We had time to reminisce as well as discuss all our plans for the future."

The two men exchanged glances, shared faint smiles. What dreams did these two vibrant men hold? Debra wondered, and felt a pang of regret that she would never know if they came true.

It was like switching a dial on a T.V. set and watching one episode of a soap opera. She knew nothing about the beginning, nor would know the ending, but she was already interestingly involved in the segment being viewed.

"I hate to say we must eat and run," Marc said when they finished their coffee. "We still have a ways to go but I promised Debra a look around as well at the horses, so we better get moving."

She was given a tour of the immediate area—the clean, well-kept out buildings, the fenced paddocks and finally the stable where Sally and the newcomer were stalled.

The foal was engagingly funny as he tried out his long legs under his mother's tolerant observation.

"How adorable!" Debra cried. "It's the first newly born foal I've ever seen."

"Then you'll have to name him," Ken said indulgently.

Marc watched her with amusement as she cocked her head to study the wobbling newcomer.

"Nothing glamourous," he warned. "I'm afraid he's not star quality. He was lazy about being born and now is too stupid to know how to nurse."

"Then he'll need a special name so he'll have something to inspire him. You've already given him an inferiority complex about lagging behind," she protested. "The poor thing is really mixed up, isn't he. He looks odd with that jet black head and multicolored body.

"I know!" she cried with sudden inspiration. "I name him Jet. Short for Jet Lag!"

The men let out a roar of laughter, scaring the foal into losing its precarious balance.

"Come on, Ken," Marc chuckled. "We better show him where to nurse so he can manage to live under that name!"

Once shown the source of food, the animal went eagerly to work.

They walked to the corral where a dozen horses were busy at a pile of hay a ranch hand had just tossed to them. They raised nervous heads at their approach, still skittish in their new quarters.

Ken pointed out the better features of the newly acquired horses. They were small in comparison to the blooded ones Debra had ridden at the riding academy, but there was a stocky strength about them that promised dependable service.

Debra strolled away, leaving the men to their technical talk. She followed the fence to get a better view of one of the horses which had caught her eye.

She was a handsome filly. Her coat shone in the sunlight, the color almost a duplicate of her own sable hair. A white blaze slashed down her chest.

"Oh, you beauty!" Debra crooned. "You're a princess forced to share quarters with peasants!"

The animal's head came up and she stared haughtily at Debra from alert brown eyes.

"Are you too proud to come and say hello?" she continued in a sing-song voice. "You know we can be good friends. Come over, baby, and let me rub your nose."

The horse pawed the ground while nervously tossing her head, resisting the pull of the soft voice.

"I'm sorry I don't have an apple for you, my pretty one, but every girl likes to be caressed. Come, baby, come and see," Debra coaxed.

The horse was quiet now under the crooning voice, her flicking ears the only indication she was aware of the girl leaning against the fence with outstretched hand. A shiver ran along her flanks and, tossing her head as if in one last gesture of defiance, she trotted slowly over to warily investigate.

Debra was thrilled with her success. She had never had the opportunity to talk a horse over like this, and to have succeeded left her trembling almost as much as the pretty mare. She moved slowly until she was rubbing the intelligent head with both hands. The horse gave a snort, then whinnying softly, showed her approval by pushing her head against Debra's shoulder.

The head jerked up, and with nostrils flaring the horse stared with apprehension as the two men walked slowly closer.

"Keep talking to her," Ken murmured. "I have some chunks of carrots you can give her."

Debra kept rubbing the silky neck while offering the tidbits. They were accepted daintily and, after some hesitation, she took some from Ken. With a final toss of her head, she trotted away.

"She's absolutely gorgeous!" Debra's face was aglow as they watched the horse run in a tight circle. "I think she's showing off for us!"

"For you," Ken amended. "You've made a conquest. That was a fine example of talking a horse in. It fulfills my faith in her.

"I had been warned she had some nasty treatment during her breaking in period," he explained, "but I was taken in by her lines and breeding, and made the gamble. Too bad you aren't staying longer to try her with a saddle."

He turned to his friend. "They make a good pair, don't they, Marc. Debbie's hair's a perfect match against the mare's coat. Can't talk you two into staying another day?"

Debra stared mutely at Marc, her eyes filled with longing.

He shook his head regretfully as he flicked the tip of her nose lightly with a finger. "Turn off that voltage," he ordered. "There's still a long ride ahead of us. I'd like you to arrive at the ranch while there's still daylight."

Just before leaving the two men became involved over a new antibiotic for horses. Debra grabbed the opportunity to run to the corral for a last goodby to the filly that had stolen her heart.

The horse saw her coming and whinnied before trotting over. There was no need to talk her in again. The attraction was mutual as Ken had observed.

"I stole an apple for you, you beauty," she murmured. "I'm sorry to have to say good-by. It would have been heaven to test the wind with you!"

She rested her head against the mare's neck, feeling silly over the tears smarting her eyes.

"One of the first things a rancher's wife learns," Marc said from behind her, "is not to become personally attached to the animals."

Debra kept her back to him, hoping he wouldn't notice the surreptitious swipe at her eyes. No such luck. His hands went to her shoulders to turn her around, and he shook his head ruefully over a tear sliding slowly down her cheek.

"You ninny," he said softly as he cupped her face and gently wiped away the evidence with a thumb. "Are you always this softhearted?"

"She got to me for some reason," Debra confessed, embarrassed over being discovered so emotional. "And I don't believe your statement. I bet you have a horse that is special to you!"

The corners of his eyes crinkled. "Touché!" he said, then took her hand. "Come, that ride is still ahead of us."

She gave one last pat to the horse and walked back to the truck with him. He didn't release her hand until she said her good-bys to the friendly couple.

She had liked them immensely and felt regret that she would never see them again, or know if they were blessed with the hoped for son.

"Check your cooler, Marc," Abby said in farewell. "I put in some slices of that coconut cake you enjoyed so much last night. I thought you'd like some for lunch."

Not until they stopped to eat did they discover Abby had also sent a bottle of wine.

"What an elegant picnic," Debra said as he refilled her glass.

Marc grinned. "I'm sneaking up on you," he said with a conspiratorial smirk. "You wished for wine and candles, remember? The candlelight comes next."

"I see where I'll have to watch you," Debra said with mock apprehension as she looked doubtfully at the refilled glass. "Would you believe one glass is usually my limit? I start floating after that."

He lifted an eyebrow, "I'll have to file that interesting information for the future. But this is only a light wine. Surely it won't affect you, especially after eating."

"I'm thirsty enough to tempt fate," she admitted, taking a sip. And by the time they had finished the cake, she found the glass empty.

It might be a light wine, but Debra soon found it still had the usual deplorable result. She fought the desire to giggle and strove to keep a stern hold on her flighty emotions. How horrible if Marc saw her on the edge of inebriation! It was silly how only wine did this to her.

The sun heated the air and, feeling exceptionally warm, she removed her jacket and tossed it into the cab. Marc started to gather the picnic things and Debra assisted with studied concentration. If she could keep a clamp on her whirling emotions for the next hour, the lightheaded sensations would fade and Marc would never know.

A breeze found them, ruffling their hair. It also found a loose napkin and lifted it up to send it flying gaily across the field. Its happy flight found a responsive cord in Debra and she ran after it, making ineffectual grabs at it as the breeze sent it on its capricious way. She began to giggle, and when she finally caught the errant napkin, she collapsed to the ground to laugh helplessly, envisioning the silly spectacle she must have made dashing after the paper.

Marc went to her, shaking his head in bemused wonder. "You really meant it about the wine!" he cried, grinning.

He bent over, slipping his hands under her arms to help her up. In doing so, his face came close to hers and their eyes met. Debra's laughter stilled, and she lifted her hand to touch his cheek.

He sank to the ground beside her as their lips met. Debra found the intoxication of their long kiss more potent than the wine. She was conscious of a devastating feeling of loss as he reluctantly pulled away from her.

"Come, you crazy kid," he said huskily, helping her to her feet. "This time, I mean it. I intend to reach the Double R while there is still daylight."

Hand in hand they walked to the truck. He opened the door for her, and she settled back in her seat with a sigh. Marc went around to the other side and slipped into the driver's seat. Switching on the ignition, he put the truck in gear and swung onto the road. When Debra stole a look at him, he appeared to be totally concentrated on his driving, his eyes firmly fixed on the distance ahead.

Now the scenery became more dramatic. The mountains thrust sharply toward the sky with traces of early snow frosting the tops. The gold splash of aspens was vibrant against the somber green of the pines. Marc pointed to a feathery spill of water with a series of rainbows at each pause down the mountain. Debra made him stop to capture it on film.

They entered a quiet valley with its inevitable river meandering through countless oxbows, and Marc announced they would soon see the Double R. The quiet pride in his voice caused Debra to examine his profile. A subtle change had come over him. A new aliveness lit his features.

"There she is," he said finally as they topped a rise.

The mountain soared ahead of them. At first glance it seemed no different from any of the hundreds they had passed, then she noticed how it rose in steps.

"It's like a giant staircase," she said in amazement.

"That's what makes it special. Each level is a plateau with excellent pastureland. You can see how perfect that is for grazing. The sides look barren from here, but those plateaus are the envy of other ranchers."

"Does the property run into this valley?" she asked, seeing a combine going through a field and belching out bales of hay.

"Only a few miles along the base of the mountain. There are farms along the river. The main crops are hay and potatoes."

"Ah, yes, the famous Idaho potatoes," Debra said.

Marc turned into an auxiliary road and soon the high gateposts proclaimed they had finally arrived at the Double R Ranch.

Chapter Four

"How far in do we go?" Debra asked as Marc crossed the iron cattle grid onto the gravel road.

"A little over two miles," he answered.

She noted the well-tended, five-rail fence lining the drive. The place had a neat, prosperous appearance. On one side heavy black Angus cropped the grass while white-faced Herefords were on the other.

"Are they the two breeds of cattle here?" she asked.

"We were handling only the Herefords until last year. A ranch closed down and we brought in those Angus. These are our feeding lots and they're being fattened for market. You'll see the difference between these that are ready and the cattle coming down.

"My brother Ray studied animal husbandry and this is his baby. For now, anyway." A trace of bitterness came into his voice and Debra looked at

71

him questioningly. But he didn't explain what was evidently a family problem.

They turned a bend in the drive and the ranch buildings spread in front of them.

Debra pulled in a sharp breath at the beauty of the setting. A long comfortable house was protected by tall trees. Clustered to one side were several buildings, a bunkhouse and stables, then the mountain rising dramatically behind them.

The surprising element was a modern A-frame house about five hundred yards from the main house. Several huge boulders stood as sentinels while a lacy waterfall cascaded in back of it. It was perfect in its setting. The natural redwood sidings blended into the brown of the bare mountain rock. The lowering sun reflected from the front wall of glass.

"Oh, my," breathed Debra. "Do you think I could get a sneak view inside that gorgeous house?"

Marc shot her an amused glance. "I'll make a point to arrange it," he promised as he drove the remaining distance to the old homestead.

"Welcome to the Double R Ranch, Debra. Your home for at least a week," he said, braking the truck in front of the house.

She looked at the wide veranda fronted in field stone stretching the length of the house. A gray-haired gnome of a man hobbled from around the side and grinned at them.

"Welcome home, Marc," he called as the tall man stepped down. "You're back a week early!"

"I had to, Dusty," Marc returned with an answering grin. "I couldn't leave the running of the ranch in your misguided hands!"

It was evidently a running joke between the two men. Their handclasp showed a mutual respect.

"Is Joyce home?" Marc asked.

"Naw. She took the two boys to visit her folks for two weeks," he replied.

Marc's eyes changed from blue to steely gray.

"Where's Ray?" he asked next.

"Up at the top corral," he answered. "He took the boys there to get an early start with the branding."

"I told him he should wait until I got back!" Anger flared in Marc's voice. "Did he think me an invalid?"

"Heck no! It was because Pawson had another heart attack and he promised to help round up his cattle as soon as you were finished here."

The stern lines in Marc's face softened. "Poor Pawson. I guess that means he'll have to sell the ranch now. He'll hate moving into town."

"Yeah. But the missus will be happy. Her arthritis has been acting up and a smaller place will suit her fine."

"Well, that puts me back to work with a vengeance. I'll have to go up tomorrow and help them so we can send some men on to Pawson. His place fills up with snow pretty fast when it comes."

"That's great," Dusty said. "Then you can take up the next batch of provisions. More bad news—Pete's in the hospital, separated from his appendix, and the crew is up there without a cook. Aunt Elsie has been preparing things here and I've been running it up every other day."

"Hell, that's no way to be feeding the men," Marc exploded. "They come in roaring hungry and shouldn't have to wait to be fed. Couldn't Ray rustle up a cook someplace?"

"Not with every ranch around doing the same thing," Dusty reminded him. "You won't find any woman willing to stay up there for a week or two and cook for a bunch of starving men in those rough conditions. There are too many easier jobs around."

Debra was still in the cab of the truck listening quietly to the exchange between the two men. She shifted now and the gray-haired man looked up in surprise.

Marc held his hand to help her out before introducing her. The little man smiled as he gave her a quizzical look of appreciation.

"Is Marie the only one in the house now?" Marc asked in exasperation. "I had planned to have Miss Wayfield stay with Ray and Joyce."

"Naw. Miss Joyce let her go home for a week since no one was around." A twinkle shone in his eyes. "Miss Wayfield will have to stay at your place. Aunt Elsie will be happy to have a pretty girl to fuss over!"

Marc lifted his ever-present Stetson and ran his hand through his hair.

"I didn't plan it like this, Debra," he said. "But Dusty is right, Aunt Elsie will be only too happy to see you. Come on, let's get going."

He helped her back into the truck and continued down the drive. She gasped in astonishment when he stopped in front of the house she had admired from the distance.

"This can't be your house!" she exclaimed in astonishment as he helped her up the broad steps and opened the door. This was no ordinary house. It could only belong to the owner of the ranch.

"Marc!" she stormed, her eyes glaring accusingly at him. "You've been lying to me! What did you intend to prove? You own this spread, don't you!"

He met her rising anger with a face carefully devoid of expression. "My brother and I do," he said quietly.

Her bewilderment added fire to her rage. "Was it fun to see how gullible I could be?" she cried. "Are you enjoying yourself thinking me good for a laugh? What made you carry it this far? You could have left me at Yellowstone and enjoyed yourself all the way home with that little student. I . . . is that all you think of me?" she stammered as tears of frustration rose periously near the surface.

His hands bit into her shoulders as he shook her.

"Debra, stop at once and listen to me," he said sternly. "You know how innocently it started. You were so pleased over meeting a cowboy I saw no reason to elaborate at that time. I never thought we'd see each other again. You were comfortable with me as an ordinary cowboy. Would you have come with me if I told you the truth at that point? I doubt it. Seeing that truck I lived in you'd have called me a liar."

Debra gulped, seeing the truth behind his words.

"And, Debra," he continued more softly, "don't ever imagine I'd laugh at you. With you, yes. You're fun to be with, but not to make fun of."

She met his piercing blue eyes and the remnants of anger melted away.

"It was so unexpected," she faltered. "I guess I overreacted."

His hands moved along her throat, doing intricate things to her pulse.

"If that was a sample, I'd hate to see you get really angry at me," he murmured as his face came closer to hers.

"Yoo-hoo! Did someone just come in?" A woman's voice called from the back of the house.

Marc gave a soft oath as he dropped his hands. "Yes, Aunt Elsie, I'm home," he answered.

"Marc, you're back early! Why didn't you call so I could have made your favorite dessert?" She stopped short upon seeing Debra. She made no attempt to hide her surprise as she raised a cheek for Marc's kiss.

He placed his arm around the woman. "Aunt Elsie, I want you to meet Debra Wayfield, who rescued me when my leg gave out. When I found she always wanted to visit a working ranch, I invited her here. Debra, my Aunt Elsie."

Marc had referred to her as the cook but Debra now realized she was a relative. The twinkling blue eyes were remarkably similar to her nephew's.

She put out both hands and clasped Debra's in a warm greeting. "My, I didn't know you had such good taste, Marc! Welcome to the Double R, Debra. I must have known company was coming. I have a Chicken Kiev ready to go in the oven."

"Will you take her up to the room next to yours, Aunt E.?" Marc asked. It's been a long dusty ride. I know Debra will appreciate a shower. I'll bring her things up."

In her first shocked anger, Debra had not noticed the inside of the house. Now she glanced around quickly. Her eyes widened in appreciation.

The living and dining room occupied the whole length of the house. A cathedral ceiling arched above, with the front of the house composed mostly of glass windows soaring the two stories. A huge fireplace faced in natural stone filled one end. Four doors opened off the balcony and Aunt Elsie led her to one of them.

The bedroom was decorated in warm yellows accented in burnt orange. The window framed the mountain and the waterfall she had seen as they arrived. Clinging precariously where the water started to cascade was a huge boulder.

"What a fascinating view!" she exclaimed, moving to the window to enjoy the scene.

"Yes, I thought Marc planned well when he built here three years ago when Ray and Joyce were married. Marc saw how Joyce loved antiques and gave up his half of the homestead so she could properly display her collection. We were certain he was building for a wife also, but nothing happened," she said with a motherly sigh.

"There's a connecting bath with the next bedroom. Take your time, dear. We eat in two hours but usually share a relaxing drink beforehand."

Debra was still drinking in the view when Marc brought in her bags. "You've captured a bit of heaven," she sighed, turning a glowing face to him. "What do you call that perfectly delightful fairy waterfall?"

"You just named it," he said, joining her by the window. "It's known locally as Reede's Fall but I secretly named it Fairy Falls when I was a little kid. Wait a few minutes and you'll see why."

They stood silently side by side as the setting sun turned the cascading water into gold threads dancing with red highlights while the rock behind changed to midnight blue. Then, as if a shade was drawn, the colors disappeared in the evening gloaming.

She raised eyes still dazzled by the colors and Marc smiled.

"It's special in the moonlight also. It looks like silver hair."

"The moon should be full this week," she said eagerly.

Marc frowned. "I would like to be here when you first see it, but I should help my brother get the mustering done. They weren't supposed to start until next week." He smiled ruefully. "Things aren't going quite as planned."

"Don't worry, Marc. I'm not exactly a guest. I more or less invited myself here and I'll find plenty to keep myself occupied. You won't be happy staying here knowing you're needed at the top corral. I'll have your Aunt Elsie tell me where to explore. Besides, if you still are offering that horse, it will take several days before I get used to the saddle again."

He moved closer to her. "We'll work out something. Meanwhile I better head for my shower."

She wished he wouldn't run his finger across her cheek that way. It immobilized her, causing all thoughts of resistance to disappear. He bent his head and for a moment she felt his warm mouth on hers before he left, closing the door behind him.

Debra hurriedly hung her clothes in the closet while deciding she would dress up for this, her first dinner in Marc's home. Her wardrobe was limited but she did have a long wraparound wool skirt in a green plaid. With it went a matching solid green knit shell with a deep scooped neckline.

Her freshly shampooed hair gleamed as she brushed it. She decided to let it fall loosely over her shoulders. At work she kept it pulled back in a neat chignon but she loved the feeling of it sweeping freely across her shoulders.

Standing on the balcony she had an unobstructed view of the room below and paused to admire the dining–living arrangement. The thickly piled rug reminded her of the tawny hair of its owner. Two inviting sofas bracketed the fireplace, now lit and sending out a warm glow. Cosy groupings of furniture offered no clutter to the grand feeling of space. At the other end by the kitchen was the dining area and Debra saw Aunt Elsie had already set the table for three.

She was halfway down the stairs when Marc stepped out of his room off the living room. He was handsome in light gray slacks with a navy blazer. The pale blue shirt had a leather thong necktie held by a silver and turquoise slide in an Indian design.

Debra was relieved she had dressed for the occasion, especially when she saw his lingering gaze of approval as she continued down the stairs. She met him by the fireplace.

"You must have missed this when you tried to get warm in your sleeping bag," she smiled in greeting. "If I had known you had this heavenly house, I'd have been convinced you were doing penance!"

"Never that," he said, opening a cabinet to reveal a built-in bar.

"I haven't said how attractive you look tonight, Debra," he murmured, handing her a glass.

"Thank you." She smiled. "That suit does things for you also. You look very much master of all you survey."

His gaze lingered over her. "I like your choice of words, Debra. I'll remind you of them one day."

Debra felt the heat rise to her cheeks and was thankful Aunt Elsie chose this moment to enter and demand her sherry.

The maid announced dinner and they strolled over to the attractive table. Debra couldn't suppress a glance at Marc. Wine glasses *and* candles!

"I swear I didn't order them," Marc said as he held her chair after seating the older woman. "Aunt Elsie is going all out to impress you."

"Dusty says you've been preparing the meals here for him to take up every other day," Marc said when they retired in front of the fireplace with their coffee. "Thanks for filling in, Aunt E."

"It's not the solution," Aunt Elsie admitted, "but it's the best we could do under the circumstances. I have Sophia cook what we can down here so it just has to be reheated. Dusty says they're managing but it isn't ideal. I have roasted a bunch of chickens to go up tomorrow. I understand you plan to take them. Do you think it's wise to put that strain on your leg?"

"If it gives out I'll be reduced to cook," he said grimly.

The sound of a phone ringing interrupted the conversation and Marc hurried through a door Debra assumed led to his private quarters.

"That's the relay phone," Aunt Elsie explained. "Ever since Dusty broke his leg at the top corral and was unable to get help for several days, Marc had that crank affair put in with instructions to whoever is there to call each night by eight. The men appreciate that precaution."

"Is the lack of a cook a severe problem?" Debra asked.

"Yes," she admitted. "They do hard work all day and the men are pretty empty when they get in. I guess Ray sends someone in early to get the food ready."

"That means three hot meals have to be prepared?"

"Actually, only breakfast and supper, and a pile of sandwiches. They pack those in their saddlebags for lunch."

Marc returned, a frown creasing his forehead. "That was Ray begging for help. Bill was assigned to breakfast detail and burned all the eggs. I hope you have a few dozen extra for me to take along."

"I'll tell Sophia to pack more," Aunt Elsie said with a sigh. "I tried to talk her into going as cook but she flatly refused to sleep outside in a sleeping bag."

"I could set up a cot for her in the kitchen," he said hopefully but his aunt's expression dashed the idea.

Debra walked to the fireplace and turned to stand in front of him. "Marc, I have a solution if you have a spare sleeping bag," she started tentatively. "I should be able to cope with cooking for your men. If you have patience for a day or two until I get the feel of it."

"No way," he said firmly. "It can be a little rough at times. It's no place for a city girl like you."

Aunt Elsie gave a gentle snort. "Now you're being silly, Marc. Your mother used to go with your father before you boys were born. Your father was only too happy to have her and she always said she enjoyed the experience!"

"You said you were sorry you couldn't show me around," Debra pointed out eagerly. "To see you bring in the cattle and brand the calves would be the highlight of my visit."

"Debra's offering a godsent solution," Aunt Elsie added. "You heard Ray moan about conditions. You're really being one man short if someone has to be appointed to cook. At least it's worth a try!"

His frown showed his resentment over the pressure applied by the two women. "No," he repeated. "I didn't invite Debra here to work, and it is hard work wrestling with a wood stove. It's entirely different from cooking in a modern kitchen."

Debra said no more. Marc had made his position clear. If she could only convince him that to actually see cowboys at work would more than compensate for any inconvenience!

The evening was still young when Aunt Elsie rose resolutely. "I'll check that Sophia has everything ready in your pickup, Marc. What time are you leaving in the morning?"

"I plan to be on the trail by five," he answered. "I have to get these eggs up to them and I'll try my hand at breakfast this one time so they can sleep a little longer."

"Isn't it still dark at that hour?" Debra asked. "How far is it to the top corral?"

"It isn't the distance as much as the road," he replied. "Going by horseback would almost be faster except I have all these provisions. Do they have Shadow with them?" he asked his aunt.

"I believe so," she answered. "I heard Ray discussing it, then deciding they might need him as a replacement."

"Good. Then I don't have to trail him behind the truck."

They spent a relaxing hour by the fireplace. Marc obliged her with some of the history of the ranch when she couldn't resist asking questions.

"The spread had always been called the Double R," he explained. "My father and uncle pooled their money and bought in partnership. The R, of course, stands for our name—Reede. When my father and mother married five years later, Uncle Roger left and went to California where he did well with a general store that blossomed into a chain of department stores. Dad eventually bought out his interest in the ranch."

"That's a switch, from rancher to store owner," Debra said in surprise. She couldn't see his nephew being happy with that change. This ranch was very much a part of him.

For at least an hour more he described to his absorbed audience the details of ranching life. Finally, he rose and stretched. "Much as I hate to, I have to say good night now. It's not that often that I have such an appreciative listener, but I saw some letters on my desk that I have to get out, and I must pack some gear for my early start. If you want to come up one day, I'll have Dusty bring you when he delivers supplies. Wait until we have all the strays in and are ready to start branding. I've told Dusty to saddle White Star whenever you want to try her.

Only remember, always tell someone where you are heading. This is big country and it's easy to get lost, so stay on the trails. I refuse to worry about you."

He paused, and Debra broke in eagerly, "Don't worry, Marc. I'll take care. And thank you for this opportunity."

He closed the space between them to place a hand along her face. "I'll stay only a few days to see how things are going. This isn't Ray's job. It's my responsibility and I can't let him handle it alone. I'll be down then to get a few days in to show you some of my special places."

He walked her to the graceful staircase and she felt his eyes follow her until she reached the balcony.

Aunt Elsie came out of her room and paused to smile at the girl. "I thought I heard you come up and wondered if you wanted something to read. It's too bad that Marc has to help Ray, but I suppose he feels he'd better check on things. Ray isn't the devoted cattleman his brother is and doesn't always pay attention to details. Not that he isn't good in other things," she added loyally.

"Then it isn't right for him to spend his time cooking!" Debra said sharply. "I wish he wasn't so adamant against me helping with that chore. I tried to convince him I would enjoy the experience."

"That's Marc for you," his aunt sighed. "Your help would be a blessing but he has a stubborn streak, and once he makes a decision he doesn't know how to back down. Still, I can see why he doesn't want his guest to work."

Her chubby face folded into a reminiscent smile. "His father was the same way."

"You mean he backs down when faced with the inevitable?" Debra asked.

"Usually." She laughed. "He always surprised us that he can be amenable in spite of his original protests."

"Do you have another sleeping bag available?" Debra asked cautiously.

"We have several in the storeroom. Shall I pack one in the truck?" the woman asked, grinning.

Debra nodded. "If you think I can get away with it."

"I'll leave that to you, my dear," she said as she went on her mission.

Debra set her alarm for four-thirty. She had to tiptoe outside, past the kitchen where Marc was making a quick cup of coffee. She slipped her roll of clothes in the back of the already laden truck and closed the cab door carefully, making the minimum of noise. She pulled her quilted jacket tight around her, shivering against the cold leather of the seat, wishing she had the courage to get some coffee. The days were still warm but the nights dipped near freezing.

His astonishment was complete when he opened the cab door. "Debra! What in the world are you doing there freezing!" he exploded.

"I'd be warmer if you closed the door," she said, smiling weakly. Suddenly her brash act didn't seem so smart. "And don't stand there or we'll never get breakfast made on time."

"Where in the hell do you think you'll sleep? We don't have beds up there. Believe me, it's basic camping. We sleep outside around the campfire and are without any conveniences. The only place under cover is the kitchen and mess hall and that's only a log cabin."

"Your aunt gave me a sleeping bag," she said. "Please, Marc, let me try. If I'm too much of a nuisance, I—I promise to leave with Dusty when he comes up." Her eyes were luminous.

He lifted his hat to run his hand through his hair. "Debra, someday your eyes will get you in a pile of trouble," he sighed. "All right. If you're so bent on seeing life in the raw, we'll take off. Hang on. It's a rough ride."

It was impossible to talk as he concentrated on avoiding the worst of the ruts. It was a slow painful ride in the dark, the headlights darkening the potholes into mysterious traps.

Debra couldn't hide her sigh of relief when they topped the last rise and she saw the rough cabin ahead. In spite of clinging for support, she felt bruised all over. The sun was barely tinting the east when he pulled up to the door.

He pointed to the dark mounds spread out in a radiating circle from a smoldering campfire.

"We'll let them sleep a little longer," he whispered. "They deserve another hour of sack time."

He hoisted a cardboard container of food and headed for the cabin. Debra grabbed her sleeping bag and roll of clothes and followed.

The mess hall was square with two long tables dominating the room. He strode past through an adjoining door. After quickly depositing her clothes in a corner, she hurriedly followed.

He lit a kerosene lamp. The kitchen surprised her.

A large old-fashioned iron stove dominated one side. Shelves stacked with heavy china lined another. But it was the size of the pots and pans that made her eyes bulge. She felt a quiver of apprehension. What had she let herself in for?

Marc must have sensed her doubts. His gaze was mocking. She gave him a brave smile.

"I'll watch you get the stove going this first time so I can learn its idiosyncracies."

She stared aghast at the two huge enameled coffeepots on the back of the stove. How did one measure to find out how much to put in them?

Marc stepped out the back door and brought in an armload of wood. "Do you know the rudiments of laying a fire?" he asked brusquely.

Debra nodded. "I was a girl scout and we all had to make an outdoor fire. But that is different from this stove."

"Very. You have to learn how to work the dampers," he said.

She watched him carefully and when the flames shot up, he adjusted the draft of the chimney. In no time the heat radiated into the kitchen and Debra held out her hands, grateful for its warmth.

"I don't want you lifting these coffeepots when they are full," he instructed. "For your information, it's one pound of coffee to a filled pot. I hope they have set them up. We do it after dinner when we can see our way to the stream."

Debra stared sharply at him to see if he was teasing.

"Camping in the rough, remember?" he said harshly. "You wanted to try it. The water is pure.

We do have a cistern but we save that for washing. The stove heats it and we do have a shower of sorts. We are careful to use it sparingly so there's warm water for all."

He opened a large refrigerator. "We have a generator that keeps this reasonably cold when we're up here. You'll find the bags of potatoes and root vegetables in the back shed. The other vegetables are in cans which makes it easier.

"There are also bins of flour and other necessities. The men did love Pete's hot rolls at mealtime. I bet they miss them."

"We'd better concentrate on breakfast first, don't you think?" she said, trying desperately to hide the quaver in her voice.

Afterward Debra couldn't recall how she managed to get through the morning. The big pot of water soon boiled and she dumped in whole *boxes* of oatmeal, stirring it with a paddle. Slabs of ham curled in a huge skillet and, after breaking several yolks in her hurry, she decided to scramble the three dozen eggs Marc assured her would be needed. Loaves of bread and tubs of butter were placed on the tables. As the sun brightened, the men crept out of their sleeping bags to sniff appreciatively at the aromas floating in the crisp air.

A heavier version of Marc, wearing a full beard, came in with a loud cheer. "You've had success! You found a cook!" he yelled in delight.

His grin changed to a surprised gape when Debra turned a flushed face from the hot stove. He whistled, his eyes taking in her sable hair tied back with a green ribbon, her neat figure in jeans. "Boy, you sure know how to decorate a kitchen, Marc! Where did you unearth this lovely?"

Marc gave a sardonic smile as he introduced them. "Debra Wayfield, my brother, Rayford, Ray to his friends," he said shortly.

"Well, Debbie," he greeted her cheerfully. "If you cook half as well as you look, we will be forever indebted to you. Even if you don't, just looking at you will take our minds off the charred offerings."

"That might be necessary," she returned with an answering grin. "This is my first attempt at a wood stove and I find it doesn't turn down when things are done. So far, with Marc's help, I've avoided scorching anything."

Ray was a friendly person. There was no evidence of the proud shaft of steel noticeable in his brother.

The word was soon out a cook had been found. After the first startled glances in the kitchen, the men hurried away to return to the table freshly shaved and with hair slicked wetly back.

There were many helping hands when she ladled out the oatmeal and passed the platters of hot scrambled eggs and juicy ham slices.

Marc filled several pitchers with coffee for easy handling and Debra poured herself a mugful, suddenly realizing this was the first she had since getting up that morning.

She watched in amazement as the piles of food disappeared. She was about to relax when she realized the lunches had to be made. Quickly she buttered lines of bread slices and piled the rest of the ham on top. Marc came in as she put the lid on the last sandwich.

"You didn't have to do that also," he said quietly when he saw the work all finished. "I was going to tackle it."

"I hope two sandwiches apiece will do," she said. "That's all the bread I could find."

He nodded as he bagged them for each man. "It's more than they deserve, the way they were eyeing you."

She looked up in surprise at the hint of—annoyance?—in his voice.

"It's only because I'm unexpected. They'll soon ignore me."

He gave a short laugh. "How little you know men!" he said as he placed the bags on the carry-through window for the men to pick up.

He ordered the men to take their dishes in for washing. The response was instant and eager. While she could laugh as she parried at their not-so-subtle comments, she was glad when Marc's tall form filled the doorway.

"All right, men" he said. "You've got your orders. Get a hustle and see if we can bring in the last of the strays today from the upper ranges."

They left, promising her the benefit of their company that evening. He watched as they left, then looked at her.

"Will you be all right, Debra? We won't be back until six. Do you think you can have dinner ready shortly thereafter?"

"I'll do my best," she assured him.

"Do you know how to shoot a gun?" he asked.

Her eyes widened at his question. "Yes. Why, are there bears in the area?"

"Not recently," he said. "There is a rifle we keep loaded for emergencies by the door. If you need any help, shoot twice. That is the distress call and we'll come as fast as we can."

He came to her and laid a finger along her cheek. "I didn't mean to frighten you," he said softly. "I just wanted to reassure you that you wouldn't be cut off from us. It can be lonely up here, Debra, when you are not used to it. Take a nap if you can. It's been a hectic day for you so far.

"And, Debra, thank you," he murmured as his lips brushed hers.

She stood enthralled until she heard the sharp clatter of hoofs on stone. She hurried to the door to see him astride a magnificent gray stallion. He leaned forward to pat the arched neck, and the two moved out to the trail where men were already fading into the distance. She strained to keep him in sight, her heart thumping. That must be Shadow, his favorite mount. How right they were for each other! Both proud and strong. Both perfect in this wild setting.

There was enough coffee for another cup and she sat down to savor it while looking resignedly at the shambles of the kitchen. First she would have to clean up before attempting to think about the night's meal.

Marc had challenged her about making rolls. How could she possibly make the quantity required by these men? There was nothing faintly resembling a cookbook in evidence.

While checking the refrigerator, she saw the pound of bars of yeast. There, on the wrapper, was the recipe for the rolls she was searching for. An hour later, the dough was set out to raise and the sack of potatoes tackled. Wearily she finished that chore, resigned to the fact she would never be able to straighten her fingers again. The chicken was already quartered and baked, needing only reheating, but if she had mashed potatoes, she needed gravy. Several large cans of chicken broth solved her problem. After browning the flour and butter to give color, she stirred in the broth plus seasonings and was pleased with the results.

When the men started returning with their strays, she realized she had not left the kitchen all day. It was too late to take a shower in the rough booth attached to the outside of the cabin, so she settled for a quick change of blouse and a gay scarf to tie back her hair. Take a nap, Marc had suggested. Hah!

Tomorrow should be easier, she assured herself. Time had been wasted this day searching for everything.

Debra was proud of the relish with which the food disappeared. A feeling of satisfied achievement welled in her when the men moved back from the table at the end of the meal and gave her a standing ovation.

"A toast to our beautiful cook!" Ray proposed, raising his coffee mug.

Debra bowed at the cries of "Hear, hear!" Forgotten were all the minor frustrations of the day.

"I think she would appreciate it more if the dishes were done for her," Marc said dryly. "Two of you fellows will take turns each evening. She has earned a well-deserved rest."

A comfortable fire was going in a ring of stones. As soon as the sun dipped behind the mountains, the air temperature dropped, and she was grateful for its warmth.

"Sit with this rock behind you," Marc said, bringing over her quilted jacket. "It will reflect the heat as well as keep the wind from your back."

He left to join his brother in having a cigarette as they walked to the corral.

The men started a parade before her that made her suppress a giggle. How like small boys eyeing the new girl on the block! The older men were quietly observant as they thanked her personally for the meal while the younger were more brash as they hunched down beside her.

"Tomorrow's my birthday," sang out one introduced as Sam. "Did they send a cake from the homestead?"

"I'm afraid I haven't seen one," Debra confessed. He seemed to be the youngest one here, probably fresh out of high school. He laughed at the hooting from the other men, but Debra caught the wistful expression in his eyes before he managed to hide it.

One fellow in his late twenties was slowly edging out the others until his shoulder was brushing hers with every movement he made. She managed to inch away on the pretense of asking if she could practice rolling a cigarette. Tom took out his pouch; his arm went around her as he attempted to guide her hands. It was such an old gambit that she giggled.

Her eye caught a movement at the other side of the fire. Even in the deepening dusk she knew it was Marc, and her heart did its usual flip as she watched his long strides bring him closer. His eyes narrowed as he took in the men clustered around her and the confident way Tom's arm encircled her.

Instinctively she pulled away and stood up. *No, Marc, I am not flirting*, she cried silently to him.

He was beside her in a few careless strides and his arm went around her waist. "I want to show you a horse I think you can safely ride, Debra," he said quietly in a voice that somehow reached every man. "I had promised you a week to explore the ranch until I found brother Ray had started up here. You're still my guest even though you volunteered to help out with the cooking."

Hands off, he was plainly saying, and the men backed away as they strolled to the corral.

Debra flushed even while acknowledging he was only doing it to keep the more predatory men away from her. If only he were really this possessive!

"I warned you they were hungry men," he said, withdrawing his arm as soon as they left the light of the campfire. "There's lean pickings in town now; most of the girls opt for more education or go off for better-paying jobs in the cities."

"That's a left-handed compliment," she said lightly, amazed over her feeling of rejection. Did he have to take his arm away so abruptly?

There was a subtle difference about him since they had come up here. Was he still angry at her for coming along? She tried to examine his face in the starlight but the wide brim of his hat held it in deep shadow. He seemed chillingly remote.

The horse was gentle as he nuzzled against Marc's chest, while searching for a treat.

"You think you can handle him?" Marc asked. "He's the gentlest one we have here. I would prefer you starting on White Star, but she's at home."

"I won't have time to ride him until I'm better organized," she confessed. "Thanks for thinking of me, Marc."

Sam had out his guitar when they returned. He was experimenting with a tune. He was still a beginner but something about the hour and the quiet rustling of the great outdoors made the hesitant notes acceptable.

When he laid down the instrument after a few abortive strains, Debra could not resist the impulse to pick it up. She tuned the strings more accurately and her fingers automatically picked out a popular ballad.

It felt good to play again. In high school she and her brother were much in demand. He would accompany on a piano or bass guitar and she would carry the melody while her husky alto augmented the tunes. They had made more than pin money playing at various functions.

She now went through part of the old repertoire, oblivious of the men around her. Her head tilted to one side and her eyes became dreamy with her words. The men sat silently as the words floated on the still air.

Debra switched from popular ballads to gospel tunes and soon had everyone's foot tapping. When the excitement of the pulsing beat started building, she moved to hymns, ending softly with the old favorite "When Day is Done."

Then, as an afterthought, she played what had

been their usual finale. It was a favorite of Debra's. Something about it filled her with a wondering yearning, and that yearning crept into her voice.

> "Oh, come, oh love of my life,
> Sing the song of the ages with me.
> The world is ours as the sun sinks
> and stars fill your eyes. I see
> the pattern of life unfold . . ."

Would she ever find the man who would stir her as these words suggested? Had she found it with this man reclining on the ground next to her? She was afraid she was stargazing too soon. Softly she finished with the repeated refrain.

> "Oh come, oh love of my life,
> Sing the song of the ages with me."

The throbbing yearning in her voice quivered through them and the men stared moodily into space. The words hung whispering in the air as she set down the guitar.

Silently they rose to spread out sleeping bags or to wander off by themselves for a last cigarette. There was no final exchange of jokes or conversation. Each was trying to come to grips with the emotions stirring, echoed hauntingly by the soft husky voice from the girl by the fire.

Debra found her sleeping bag placed between Marc's and Ray's.

"We won't go in for the luxury of night clothes," Ray informed her brusquely. "Our only concession is to remove our boots. Toward morning the extra clothes feel good. You're not used to this climate, Debbie. I'd advise you to wear your quilted jacket, or at least put it over you in the bag. That fire is a delusion.

"And, Debbie," he added as he zippered himself in, "thanks for the entertainment."

Marc was the last one to settle down. He checked the horses, then threw several logs on the fire before coming over. He squatted beside her and gazed at her upturned face.

"After all you've done today, you at least should have an inner spring mattress," he said softly. "Instead I offer you a rock-hard ground with a chance at pneumonia."

His hand went to brush away a strand of her hair the night breeze had settled across her forehead. "You constantly amaze me, Debra. Where did you ever learn to sing like that?"

"I never had formal training though I used to sing in the school glee club." She smiled up at him as she explained how she and her brother had played at different functions. It took all of her willpower not to put her hand over his where it rested on her cheek.

"A girl of many talents," he said. She wished he didn't always wear that hat. His face was in shadows and she hungered for one last examination.

"Sleep well. Don't worry about getting up early. I'll start breakfast." He zipped her in the last few inches, then bent, placing a short, hard kiss on her mouth before slipping into his bag.

She stared up at the stars pulsing in the black

velvet sky, certain she would not be able to sleep in this strange environment. The ground was hard and the small stones seemed to grow larger under her. There was so much to think over after this eventful day. She inched around a boulder and promptly fell into a deep sleep.

Chapter Five

The tantalizing aroma of coffee woke her up. Debra looked around, trying to orient herself. She struggled with the zipper on her bag, suppressing a shiver at the sharp chill in the air. The fire was a bed of gray ashes. The dark forms of the men in a rough circle around it were vague lumps in the quiet dawn.

Marc's was the only empty space. His sleeping bag was gone. She hurriedly rolled hers up and went to the cabin. A silver plume of smoke rose in the still morning air.

He was busy placing lamb chops on the large griddle when she came into the kitchen.

"That's not fair," she greeted him. "I was going to see how good I was at starting the stove."

His gaze swept over her. "I see you survived the night," he said as he poured her a mug of coffee. "This is instant, but it will feel good going down to get rid of the chills. It takes a little longer for these big pots to boil."

She accepted it gratefully, going to check the water for the hot cereal.

"I hope you didn't get too cold," he said. "It is much warmer when those bags are shared. I thought about inviting you over, but I didn't think it would help the morale of my men."

She ignored his teasing. "I admit my last thought was what to do with the pile of boulders growing under me, but I don't remember much after that."

He nodded to the bowl of leftover mashed potatoes he had put out. "Do you think you can quick fry that? It will slow them down on the bread that's left."

She quickly added eggs and milk and patted them into flannel cakes. The routine was established and she urged him to leave when everything was cooking. Tomorrow she would make certain she was up early. Marc worked hard enough without losing precious hours of sleep doing kitchen duty. He was not a boss who left the work to others. Gone was the relaxed, easygoing person she had known those first days at Yellowstone. Here was a steel-hard man in complete control. She noticed the respect the men held for him. Even his brother bowed to his authority.

When the rolls were covered to raise, she went to explore around the cabin. The fenced corral in the far section of the plateau was filling with lowing cattle. Two men were urging reluctant animals through a gate. They were too far away for her to recognize them.

Blue flowers were in bloom and she gathered some, plus pieces of flowering sagebrush. She placed them in several empty jars on the tables.

She was reminded of the wistful expression caught in Sam's eyes. He would appreciate them even though he wouldn't say anything. Was today really his birthday? She had meant to wish him happy returns but had been too busy to remember.

She returned to the kitchen and looked at the stack of baking pans. Nothing here for a multi-layered cake, but this was the time to improvise.

She looked in satisfaction at the finished product. Two large roasting pans had produced satisfying layers. These she had split and spread with strawberry jam. Covering the piled layers with a butter frosting was simple, but fancy decorations stymied her until she found some chocolate chips. She sprinkled them liberally along the edges and spelled his name down the middle. If only there were some candles! She carefully hid the confection in one of the cabinets, intending it as a surprise.

Not until the men returned did she discover a supply of candles in a metal box on one of the top shelves. They were ungainly, but would have to do. The large cake could take two of the thick candles.

The glow on Sam's face was payment for her extra work. He was overwhelmed as she carried the cake in when they finished the main meal. But more than anything was the frank look of appreciation that shone in Marc's eyes.

That night the men clamored for more songs, and after Debra taught Sam some chords, he handed her the instrument. This time she insisted on a sing-along and they called out favorites in which they all lustily joined.

Marc finally took the guitar from her amid calls of spoilsport from the men. "Besides giving Debra a rest, morning comes around fast here," he pointed out.

Debra went to fetch her sleeping bag but Marc's fingers curled around her arm and led her toward the corral. She watched him roll a final cigerette by the light of a bright moon. The flare from the match brought his features into sharp outline. His light blue eyes were on her and her lids fluttered down under their piercing regard.

"That was a very nice thing you did for Sam," he said, resting his arms on the fence. "This is his first trip here. He's just out of school and is living out his dream of being a cowboy. Don't get me wrong. He works hard or I wouldn't have him, but he still is floating between boy and manhood." A spiral of smoke curled up over his hat. "And those flowers. I don't think we've ever had flowers decorating the table before. Trying to make the shack homey?"

"Don't worry, I won't attempt curtains on the windows," she laughed, then asked questioningly, "Is my cooking all right? Am I making enough? I've never seen such tremendous appetites!"

His teeth flashed white as he smiled. "You get a gold star. The men are impressed. Pete will have to look to his laurels when he gets better."

He dropped his cigarette, grinding it carefully into the ground, and dropped his arm from the high fence to settle across her shoulders. Her heartbeat quickened as he drew her close. He paused only to flip his hat back before claiming her waiting lips. The fire ignited as his arms became steel bands binding her willing body against his.

When he finally lifted his head she fell into an aching void and rose on her toes to reclaim his lips.

With a soft groan he gave her one last hard kiss and put her away from him.

"I shouldn't have done that," he said. "It was bad enough with you in reach last night. You're a terrible temptress, O Woman of the Soft Brown Eyes." He caught his breath as he stared down at her. "Have I kissed those stars into them?"

His hands moved up her arms to fondle her neck before moving on. His fingers buried in her hair as the palms of his hands rested on her cheeks. His thumbs rubbed sensuously along her temples.

"We'd better go back," he whispered, kissing her eyes closed. "Be a good girl and don't look at me like that or we won't make it."

Her heart rebelled but common sense prevailed. Something special was happening. Something which had to be taken carefully, one day at a time.

Somehow she managed to awaken on time. The stove proved a friend, offering no resistance. Not until she turned to the table did she see the empty cake plate. The demons! There had been half a cake left. They must have polished it off before going to bed.

Under the plate was a paper. DELICIOUS! was printed in bold letters across the top and all had signed their names below.

Marc came in to see her bemused expression. She handed him the paper and he reached for the marking pen, adding his name.

"You shouldn't get up so soon," she said, handing him a mug of coffee. "I can manage now. You can stand the extra hour of sleep."

He raised a mocking eyebrow. "Perhaps I like to hobnob with the cook. Any objections?"

The flush coloring her cheeks had nothing to do with the heat from the stove.

That evening over the meal, conversation was about two carcasses they had found.

"I haven't seen any big cats around for several years," Bill, one of the older men, stated. "I heard they've been having some losses further upstate this year. I wonder if one is ranging near us?"

"You're sure you didn't see any prints or spoor?" Marc asked.

"No," Bill replied. "One was killed about two weeks ago and the other a good week ago. Too many other animals have been around sitting in on the feast."

"I saw a flash of brown in the brush when we first came up," Tom said. "I thought it was a stray and went in after it but found nothing. At the time I thought it odd. I figured I was hallucinating and forgot about it. Now I wonder if it was a big cat."

"Where did you see it?" Marc demanded.

"Up by the big split rock."

Ray nodded grimly. "That's the general area where we found the cows."

The men discussed which cartridge was best to use as they cleaned their rifles. Now they were basic men, stalking game in a world that excluded women. Their laughter was hard and purposeful. Eyes would be sharp in the morning, seeking the silent glide of a brown body ghosting through the brush.

Debra wandered away. In a small copse of aspen a lone pine rose straight to the sky. She sat in the deeper shadows cast by its branches.

Chin resting on her knees, she hugged her legs. This was ever the way of man. It was a wise woman who realized there was a time and place for everything, and now the primitive call from the hunting blood sang in their veins.

She was aroused from her reverie by the murmur of angry voices. The sound surprised her. The men had seemed so congenial. The voices were coming toward her and she rose to leave the area, first pausing to peer into the gathering darkness, curious as to who they were. There was a sharp exclamation of annoyance.

Marc! And Ray! What was causing the dissension between the two brothers? She had noticed only a strong current of affection between them.

"You have to stop being the big brother," Ray said, his voice sharp with anger. "I have a right also in how to handle our inheritance. Uncle Roger said he'd help finance the project if you gave your okay. Joyce has been busy setting up plans and I have contacted builders and other contractors to get a cost estimate."

"I refuse to have this place overrun with tourists," Marc answered. His anger was barely controlled. "I'll buy out your half if you two are so set on this idea. You can buy some bankrupt setup and pour your money into it."

"You know that would be more than I could raise at one time," Ray stormed. "Besides, all my life I've dreamed of using the other side of the mountain. You have no use for it for cattle. I won't be disturbing your watershed, if that is what is bothering you. The ski slopes are already made by landslides and natural formation. They just have to be cleaned of debris. The lake is a natural for sailing and swimming and I've looked into the feasibility of stocking some of the streams with trout.

"It's not that we're going into this blind," his voice was taut with emotion. "Joyce had an excellent business course in college and she has an aunt who was a dietician for several top hotels and is dying to come out of retirement. I've even applied for a liquor license and am pretty sure I'll get it by the time we are ready to go."

Debra had hesitated too long. Now it was too late to leave. The men stopped a short distance from her as they squared off in hot debate.

"Evidently the old homestead means nothing to you." Marc said scathingly. "Joyce keeps crying about its charm, yet you're intent on building additions that will spoil the very thing you say you want to keep."

"We need someplace to lodge the guests." Exasperation crept into Ray's voice. "We want to avoid the Swiss Chalet image so prevalent. You have to admit the homestead gives a warm welcoming feeling."

"And what about my house?" Marc said icily. "I'm too close to hope they won't be climbing all over it and looking in the windows. I'll be damned if I'll put up curtains or a fence to ruin my view.

Ray lifted his shoulders uncomfortably. "There are other spots with a better view. Perhaps we could move the house or build you a new one."

Oh no! thought Debra in horror at the suggestion. Not away from his Fairy Waterfall! Didn't Ray know that Marc, too, has his dream and where he built his home was the culmination?

"My answer is a flat no!" Marc answered. The force of his fury swept across the intervening space.

With a sharp oath of defiance, Ray turned and stalked away, leaving Marc standing rigid in the moonlight as he glared after him.

Debra watched as he rolled a cigarette and inhaled deeply. If only he, too, would go on so she could leave unnoticed! She moved cautiously, ready to go when he did. Her foot slipped. Horrified, she heard the stone as it rattled down the slight incline.

Marc whirled, the instant woodsman, alert to the foreign noise.

Debra stepped forward from the protective shadow.

"I—I didn't mean to eavesdrop, Marc," she stammered. "You came upon me so quickly, I couldn't leave."

He watched in silence as she approached. Would his anger spill over on her? His hat still hid his face in shadow but she could see tension in his body.

"It won't be a secret much longer that the Reede brothers are feuding," he said bitterly. "Especially since Ray informs me he's been active getting estimates. The word gets out fast in a small community."

"But you won't let him influence you to move your beautiful home!" she exclaimed anxiously. "Oh, Marc, you'll never find a lovelier location!"

"It's nice having you in my camp," he said. "I was beginning to think I was completely crazy. I didn't know Uncle Roger was willing to back him financially. He and Joyce have been talking about this resort idea since they were married, but I felt it couldn't get off the ground. I didn't believe a bank would lend them money in the amount they would need, and I certainly wouldn't countersign a mortgage on the spread."

"You did offer to buy him out so he could try elsewhere. That sounded like a reasonable solution."

"It would strap me right now," he admitted. "But if they feel they want to run a ski resort, I wouldn't stand in their way. But not on this ranch!"

"Is that what they want?" she asked. "I only heard the last of your conversation."

"Yes, a ski resort in the winter and a family ranch with horses and backpack setup in the summer. Can you see me existing with that crawling all over the place?"

Frankly she couldn't. This man was of the old breed. He needed open space around him to exist. Strangers making use of his territory would drive him crazy.

"Could you manage all the new projects you started if he left?" she asked. When they arrived, Marc had said the fattening station was Ray's concern.

"Of course," he said. "They were my ideas to begin with. I pushed them ahead, thinking they might stimulate Ray since that was more his field, and maybe he would give up his crazy dream."

"He isn't the cattleman you are, is he," she said softly.

"You're right, he isn't," Marc said shortly.

"It's like a repeat of your father and uncle," she continued. "Maybe he really is better cut out for a business career."

"Are you trying to be diplomatic?" he asked. A

warning hardness edged his voice and she shook her head.

"Of course not. I have no business interfering with your private affairs. I was only thinking aloud. Forgive me."

He threw his cigarette down, carefully grinding it out.

"Shall we go back? The boys will be bedding down and we may as well do likewise," he said firmly ending the conversation.

Debra walked beside him, frowning into the night over his withdrawal. She had not meant to pry into a personal problem and she searched for another subject.

"Are your men going after whatever killed your cattle tomorrow?" she asked.

"No, we don't have the time. We should be rounding up the last of the strays to brand. They are, however, taking their rifles and will keep their eyes open."

The ground didn't seem as hard that night and sleep came quickly. There was no private goodnight from Marc. She could still feel tension in the air as she settled into her sleeping bag.

Debra was even better organized the next morning. She greeted Marc triumphantly with a mug of coffee. The stove had behaved perfectly. In spite of the boasting as to how they were going to get the big cat, there was an intensity of purpose about the men as they left.

Debra wandered to the horse corral and wished she had asked Marc about a saddle for Jacko. Today was a perfect day to see how good she was at riding after the long layoff.

A canvas caravan similar to a sheepherder's shelter was standing by the fence. Upon looking in, she saw it contained extra saddles and equipment. Evidently it had been used to bring up those supplies. She soon found a saddle that looked comfortable, then leaned eagerly over the fence, waving a carrot at the horses as she whistled experimentally the way the men did.

Either the carrot or whistle worked. Several of the horses became inquisitive enough to come over. She patted them as she shared the carrots, meanwhile working Jacko into her confidence.

He was a patient horse as Marc had promised. There was no trouble saddling him and she started eagerly on a morning exploration.

After a slow trot to the main corral that contained the cattle, her rapport with the animal was complete and she turned him down a trail.

This held a better overall view of the plateau they were on. The grass and the ever-present sagebrush covered most of the area—hugging approximately five miles along the mountain and extending over two miles out. There were few trees and those mainly along the small brooks that sprang from the ground and joined before cascading into a waterfall that bounced noisily over the cliffside.

She hoped the opportunity would come to see all of the ranch. Each section was different, each with its own special scene. The horse grazed as she sat quietly in the saddle admiring her immediate surroundings. This was a good life. One she could enjoy forever.

Steady, Debra, she warned herself. He sends your pulse soaring but what do you do to him? The attraction is there, but how far does he want to commit himself beyond a flirtation? After all, you practically begged him to bring you to the ranch!

Reluctantly she turned back, passing Bill and Sam with a wave of hands as they herded some reluctant strays into the enclosure. The cattle were bawling loudly, protesting the denial of their freedom.

Tying Jacko to the hitching post in front of the cabin, she went in to set the rolls and grab a quick bite for lunch. If she hurried, she'd have time to take a short ride in the other direction before starting dinner.

She looked up as she heard the horse pawing nervously on the ground. Someone must have finished early and was coming for a cup of coffee. She reached for another mug, then hesitated. Jacko was whinnying now. It was not the soft welcome of recognition but one of fear. It sent a chill down her spine. What was going on out there?

Sunlight blinded her when she dashed to the door. She blinked against its brightness. The horse was frantic, crying shrilly as he pulled against the re-straining rein.

Then she saw it. The only movement was the twitching of its long tail as it sat crouching next to the boulder by the hitching post. The long tawny body of the mountain lion was awesome as it crouched, every inch exuding concentrated power.

Debra remembered reaching for the rifle cradled on the antlers by the door. The shot rang out as he started his leap. He somersaulted in midair and landed next to the crazed horse. With one last desperate lunge, Jacko broke the leather thongs and tore madly away.

The lion staggered to its feet, blood pouring down one shoulder. His pale yellow eyes stared at her with wild intensity before he turned to limp away.

One thing had been impressed upon Debra when taught how to shoot. Never let an injured animal go free. It was a cruel way to let a creature die, and, in the case of a predator, could turn him into a raging attacker.

Debra ran after the beast. When he paused to lick at his wound, she raised the rifle again. This time the bullet hit true and he collapsed with a sigh.

She stared blankly at the animal, unable to comprehend what she had done. She had reacted instinctively to save Marc's horse. Now she saw the beauty of the wild beast, the golden hide and the massive head. How could she have killed this symphony of power?

Then a wave of nausea hit and she leaned helplessly against a tree until the spasm finished. Not until she reached the cabin did she realize she was still clutching the rifle. She sank weakly against the sill, leaning heavily against the door.

Marc saw her first—her eyes closed, her face white, and the rifle lying in the dust at her feet. Ray was behind him, leading the reluctant Jacko by the broken reins.

Marc swung off his horse and gathered her in his arms. Debra opened her eyes to wonder briefly over his white face before burying hers in his shoulder.

"Debra, my God, Debra! Are you all right?" he cried hoarsely.

She nodded her head, not trusting her voice but content to remain in the haven of his arms.

"We heard the two shots and realized they came from this direction. Then when we spotted Jacko running with an empty saddle . . . !"

Slowly his arms relaxed and she raised her head, reluctant to leave their protection.

"I'm all right, Marc," she assured him. "It's just that I don't kill a mountain lion every day."

The two men stared at her in disbelief.

"What did you say?" It was Sam who voiced their astonishment. He and Bill had responded to the gunshots also.

She pointed a shaking finger to the far side of the clearing where the tan body was stretched. "It tried to jump Jacko and I shot it." She was appalled at the quaver in her voice. Reaction set in and her body trembled in the circle of Marc's arms.

Without a word he led her inside and made her sit on a bench. Ray followed with a flask from his saddle bag and offered her a drink.

"I—I don't need it," she protested. "I'll be all right in a minute."

Marc lifted the flask to her lips and forced her to take some. She blinked against the quick tears as the fiery liquid burned into her.

"One more," he said sternly and she was forced to comply.

"Now fill us in," he said, sitting next to her. His arm was still around her. Anxiously he watched the color return to her face.

She told them how she had heard the terror in the horse's frantic cries and spotted the lion crouching, then shot it as it sprang.

"When it tried to get away, I knew I couldn't let

113

an injured animal go, so I followed it. When it paused, I used the other shot. Did I do right?" she asked, raising worried eyes to him.

He cleared his throat before answering. "Yes, you did right, Debra. But don't get in such a situation again!" His arm tightened momentarily again before he rose to go outside.

The four men returned shortly. Young Sam's eyes were round with disbelief.

"I've never seen one this big. It's real trophy size. You should get it mounted!" he enthused.

Debra shuddered. "Spare me! There's barely enough room in my apartment for me without having him staring at me all the time! I'll never forget the look in his eyes after the first shot."

"Then you should have his hide tanned. It would make a perfect rug," he persisted.

She gave him a weak smile. "That takes more money than I can afford. You can have it if you wish."

Bill came with mugs of coffee for all. He eyed the girl with frank admiration. "You know you'll make the local papers. A lot of ranchers will be happy to hear what you've done."

"That's the last thing I would want," she groaned. "If my brother should see it, he'd have a fit and order me home!"

"What are you going to do with it?" she asked Marc. "This is rocky country and you'd be hard pressed to bury the body."

"The vultures will take care of that," Sam said. "They're circling already."

Debra shuddered.

"Don't worry, we'll pull it away," Ray assured

her. "We'll have to leave it though until the other fellows see it or they won't believe it. All their grand tales about how they were going to stalk the mighty cat and this slip of a girl beats them to it!" He chuckled. "I can't wait to see their faces!"

He put down his empty mug and rose. "Come on, men, those last few cows we gathered have no doubt scattered. We'd better get them before they get too far. This should wind things up. Branding can start tomorrow. I suppose you want to stay here?" he asked his brother.

Marc nodded. "Debra has had enough of a shock. I don't want her to be alone. I'll start on supper."

She started to protest but he silenced her with a cool glance.

She trailed him into the kitchen and insisted there was no reason she couldn't peel the potatoes. "I can do that sitting down," she pointed out. "Please, Marc. I'll feel better doing something. I admit I was shaken for a while but I'm not about to fall apart."

His blue eyes examined her face and shrugged his shoulders in resignation.

"I'll be able to cope better with the next lion I meet," she said solemnly. "It will be old hat by then."

He caught the glimmer of a smile in her eyes and his lit in response. "I can see having you around can easily bring on the gray hairs. Somehow one should be able to build up a defense," he said ambiguously. "Perhaps it would be wisest if you went back to the house when Dusty brings up the next batch of supplies."

Her eyes clouded. Did he want to get rid of her that badly? She concentrated on the lengthening peel of potato. "I thought I was doing an adequate job," she said in a small voice. "The men seem to be surviving on the food I'm serving them."

He took in her bowed head, the droop to her mouth. "They're more than surviving," he said. "They never had it so good. I'm only thinking of you, Debra. I have no right to expose you to more danger. This is no vacation for you working over a wood stove to feed these hungry men." His voice was hard again as if warning her away. "The temperature will keep dropping from now on. There was frost on the grass this morning, and the ground doesn't get any softer to sleep on. Certainly there can be no lure in that!"

She looked at the man leaning against the sink, his arms folded across his broad chest.

"But what can replace the birds waking me in the morning! Now that I've established the routine, it's not bad. There is so much yet to explore. I don't think I'll ever get tired of seeing the calves kick up their heels in play, or a mother lowing softly to one." Her eyes were dreamy. "You have a wonderful world here, Marc, and I have so little time to absorb it!"

He moved his shoulders in an impatient shrug. "You're back in your western novels again, still seeing everything through rose-tinted glasses. There can be searing droughts and killing blizzards. For one used to the city, there can be acute loneliness."

A smile curved her lips. "You don't seem to be suffering.

"I've been bred to this. It's different for me." His eyes were chips of blue ice.

"You're not discouraging me, you know." She sat up straight, squaring her shoulders. "I would like to stay up here for the rest of the time, unless you object strenuously."

He spread his hands in resignation. "How could I? As I said before, I am only thinking of your welfare."

"Good," she said crisply. "Then don't say anything more about leaving." Then, taking the bull by the horns—she grimaced at the metaphor—she stared defiantly at him. "You know I do not have to go back to work for the month. I offer my services as camp cook until you are finished here."

He stood unmoving as he heard her offer. "That's very generous of you, Debra," he said quietly. "At this point I think I had better accept your offer."

There was much whooping and hollering when the men returned and viewed the remains. They teased good-naturedly about her Amazon potential, but there was a respectful awe beneath it all.

Debra looked nervously at the spot where she had felled the animal when she later joined the men outside. She breathed a sigh of relief to see they had dragged it away and hoped fervently she would not stumble over it when out riding. She took some carrots to the corral and was happy to see that Jacko appeared to have forgotten his terror of the afternoon. He nuzzled her in greeting and munched happily on her offering.

"You're spoiling him for the boys, you know." She stiffened at the sound of his voice behind her, every nerve tingling as he came next to her to lean against the railing.

"I was checking to see if he had any ill effects," she said, rubbing her hand along his nose. "I didn't want to be the cause of his becoming nervous.

"They're a pretty tough breed. These cow ponies are used to meeting all situations."

Jacko nudged her shoulder, begging for another handout.

"Go away, you beggar." Debra laughed.

Smelling no more carrots, he gave one last push and trotted away. It caught her off guard, and she stumbled backward. Marc's arms were around her, pulling her close against his chest.

This is what I've been waiting for, she thought wildly until all coherency stopped. She was drowning in a world enclosed by steel-hard arms and muscular body. Her hands buried in his tawny hair, pushing his hat away. Pictures of the rippling muscles of the golden lion flashed though her. That is what he was. Her golden lion, and she thrilled as she pressed her soft curves against his rock-hard body.

His hand caressed her throat and trailed down, unbuttoning the front of her shirt. Her breasts leaped to life under his gentle massaging, and his mouth followed the path of his hand.

Desire was a raw flame and she moaned under its urgency. He reclaimed her lips, dropping a hand to her hip to crush her against him.

Marc heard the voices first. He raised his head, his body taut as he muttered an oath under his breath. His arms fell away. Debra hurried to button her shirt, fumbling with trembling fingers.

She blessed the moon hiding behind a cloud as she tried to still her ragged breathing. The wooden fence railings were cool bars where she leaned her hot body against them. Marc raised a boot on the lower rung next to her as he, too, leaned against the fencing. The Stetson was again pulled down, hiding his face. How could he look so cool and unperturbed? Had she only imagined he had been consumed by the same fire?

Ray and Bill came through the trees. They stopped when they saw the two by the corral.

"We were coming to check the horses before turning in," Ray said. "Didn't know you two were here."

"Debra was concerned about Jacko," Marc said. His head was bent as he concentrated on rolling a cigarette.

The men talked over the next day's branding and Debra started to leave. Marc dropped a restraining hand on her arm and she leaned back.

"You coming to watch the branding?" Ray asked. "It's not the romantic sight of paintings. It's dusty and noisy and smells of burnt flesh," he warned her. "My wife gets sick over the whole idea and usually takes off to visit her family."

"I don't know how I will react," Debra admitted honestly. "I'll come as soon as I get the kitchen under control."

The two men left and they remained motionless until he finished his cigarette. What was this tall man thinking? Was he sorry to have given in to his emotions . . . and worse, did he think she abandoned herself like this to all men?

Never had her body taken over like this. Never had she flamed with such desire.

"We better get back, Debra," he said, moving away. "We'll be needing breakfast by daybreak. If all goes well, we'll get most of the branding done tomorrow and finish off the next day. Then we separate them into two drives. It takes two days to get them settled in winter pasture."

She walked silently beside him, staring ahead with unseeing eyes as they entered the small stand of trees. A root tripped her, and steel fingers steadied her.

"That was clumsy," she mumbled, wondering why her throat was so tight and tears were pushing threateningly behind her lids.

"It's hard to see," he admitted, then stopped. His hand restrained her and she turned, trembling from his touch.

His hands went to her shoulders and then traveled gently up to cup her face. The moon bathed her in silver, turning her eyes into black pools as they gazed searchingly up at him.

"You pack a wallop of a kiss, you know," he murmured. "I'm not apologizing for what happened back there. I'm only sorry we were interrupted."

His face came down and she thought, *I shouldn't let this happen again*, as his lips covered hers. It started as a light good-night kiss, but their lips clung hungrily and she again was crushed in his arms.

"This is getting to be a habit," he said thickly against her mouth. "It has to stop right now. I'm only human, woman."

He gave her one last hard kiss, bruising her mouth, then held her away. "It's going to be hell having you sleep an arm's reach from me," he

muttered. "Get going. I'm having one last cigarette."

He gave her a gentle push toward the campfire.
She floated away on feet that didn't quite touch the
ground. So he wasn't immune after all! He felt the
same magical pull!

Chapter Six

Debra decided to take the men a cooling drink. The only container large enough was the big pot used for cereal and soup. She brought up the half-truck and set it in the back. Ice cubes layered the bottom and she dumped in bottles of concentrated lime and orange juice. Two pails of water and generous scoops of sugar brought it to the right flavor. The lid would help prevent it from sloshing over the side while driving over the rough ground. Mugs went into a cardboard box, and off she went.

She sat in the car trying to see through the dust. Her nose wrinkled against the hot odor of burning hair and flesh.

In the larger corral the cows were lowing in distress. Their calves were jammed into a smaller enclosure. One by one they were forced down a narrow chute. They were pressed against the bars when they reached Marc. The hot iron came down on a rump. A small spiral of smoke rose up. At the same instant, Ray gave the animal an injection and an ear was nicked. The bawling calf was then pushed along to be dumped into a large vat of vile-smelling tick dip. They were then herded into another corral away from the cows. Their life with their mother was over. In a few days they would forget that extra treat of milk and live off the winter grass.

Beneath the blazing sun, the men worked stripped to the waist, their muscles rippling in their broad shoulders and arms. It could have been a scene from a classic frieze.

Marc was the first to see her and she lifted a mug to indicate she had something for them. For a moment he stood, a statue bronzed by the sun, tawny head proudly lifted, broad shoulders thrust back. Even from the distance she could see the rise and fall of his magnificent chest as he breathed deeply from the exertion of his work.

He called out an order and they finished with the calf before coming noisily to quench their thirst. But her eyes were still dazzled from the sight of him as she kept ladling from the pot.

"Boss, you better sign her up for next year," one of the men called out as he chewed on an ice cube. "You won't have any trouble getting men when they find you have her to spoil them."

Marc gave her a mocking glance. "It's a good idea. I'll keep it in mind if she's still around."

It struck like a physical blow. *If she were still around!* So it had only been a summer romance after all.

She gathered the mugs as the men went back to

work. They all thanked her profusely, but Marc only nodded his head before striding off. Not once had he spoken to her.

She crawled into the cab to lick her wound. Was this only an interlude for him? No, she thought fiercely. There was something special, something that sang between them.

Her hands, clenched tightly around the wheel, hurt and she looked at them in wonder. She finally faced the truth. She loved him. Just like that. He had walked into her heart and taken possession and she knew there was no way she could ever evict him.

She tried to be objective. Yes, he was attracted to her. Yes, their kisses had roused him as much as her. But those damning words lay coldly across her heart. *If she were still around!* He was planning no future with her.

Had she made a mistake by maneuvering him to let her come up here? She had been the aggressor and he was not the man to like a woman to take the lead. Had she been too available? She had succumbed, melting in his arms and offering him no challenge.

That night she made certain she stayed within the ring of the fire. She picked up the guitar and had the men singing. Sam sat like an adoring puppy at her feet. She even encouraged Tom, the self-proclaimed lady killer. She laughed up into his face over his jokes, even fluttered her eyelashes once or twice.

And all through her performance her heart was aware of Marc standing in the shadows beyond the glow of the fire. She saw the pinpoint light of his cigarette, and the men drifting over to speak with him awhile before leaving.

Look, Marc, I'm not running after you anymore. It's up to you to make the next move, she silently spoke to him.

The sleeping bags were unrolled and it was a subdued girl who crept into hers. Marc had not spoken to her all evening. There was no whispered good night when he stretched his long form next to hers.

Debra stared into the star-filled sky. She could not keep up this charade. She could never mask her feelings. Marc would have to take her the way she was. Or leave her. And after tonight's performance, it looked as though it would be the latter.

Debra might have decided to forego her act, but Marc seemed to have reached a decision of his own. His good morning was no warmer than that he gave to his men. He treated her as though she were one·of his employees.

She made lemonade again and included a pot of hot coffee for their lunch. This time she did not wait to serve them. She left the truck where they'd see it and walked the short distance back to the horse corral and whistled for Jacko. He came eagerly for her proferred carrot.

She rode long and hard, stopping frequently to admire the ever-changing view and to give the horse a breather.

Goodbye mountain, she cried. *You're beautiful in your ruggedness and it hurts to leave you. I'm already in love with you. Goodbye, you dainty little waterfall. You're not my Fairy Falls, but I could have loved you as much if given a chance.*

They had emptied the pot of coffee and finished the lemonade by the time she returned. The work was in full swing after their lunch break, and if he saw her, he gave no sign though the men nearby waved cheerfully as she drove away in the truck.

Debra decided to bake another fancy cake for dessert. This was the last supper they would all be together. Part of the cattle would be taken down the next day by most of the men, and the rest would follow the day after.

She made chocolate and vanilla cakes in the big roasting pans then sliced them through the middle to create alternate dark and light layers. She cooked a custard and stirred strawberry jam in to bind the layers. A fluffy frosting went over it, decorated with curls of dark chocolate. It was a masterpiece and was her swan song. She did not know if he would leave with the first or second shift, or with which one she would be ordered out.

The men were enthusiastic with their praise. The thick slices disappeared quickly.

Debra sat precariously on the hitching post afterward, not wanting to join the men around the fire. If she did, they'd beg her for some songs, and she didn't feel like singing. Marc had eaten his full share of the cake but had not joined in the praise. Didn't he know it was a peace offering . . . a love offering?

Ray came over and leaned against the post. "The boys won't forget what you have done," he said with a smile. "That cake is what starts folk stories. Years from now when they get together, the talk will always come around to Debbie and that fabulous cake she made. It will grow mightily in the telling."

Her laugh rang out, surprising her. She didn't know there was any lightness left in her.

When he left, the restlessness built up and she had to move. She gathered the last of the carrots and started toward the corral. She reached the little copse of trees when she became aware of footsteps behind her. He was following her!

She turned eagerly, and the man stepped forward. Her disappointment was shattering.

"Saw you heading this way and thought you might like company," Tom said. "A pretty thing like you shouldn't be wasted on a moonlit night like this. Checking the horses?" he asked, seeing the carrots in her hands.

"I'm giving them a last treat." Darn him, why did he have to follow her! Suddenly it became important he did not join her by the corral. The place was sacred. She could not share it with him.

He reached for her arm but she pulled away, ashamed how she had flirted with him the night before.

"Will you do me a favor, Tom?" she asked in a tight voice. "I'd like to be alone. No offense, of course. I just want to say goodbye to the horses by myself."

He stared at her then shrugged his shoulders. "I can take a hint when it's thrown at me. I just thought after the way you acted last night you weren't the Big Boss's private property anymore. Far be it from me to step on his private preserve. Whatever game you're playing, it's working. He hasn't been able to keep his eyes off you." He turned sharply and went back to the fire.

Debra stood there, unable to move. Was what he said true? No. She had heard hurt male pride in his voice.

"Did you mean it when you said you wanted to feed the horses alone?"

This time there was no doubt about the deep-timbred voice. Marc stepped out of the shadow of a tree.

"Not really," she admitted breathlessly.

He did not touch her as they turned to continue the walk. He did not have to. She was vibrantly aware of him striding beside her. Every nerve tingled. Even the hairs on her arms seemed to stand up. He was here—with her! She prayed nothing would mar this miracle.

Jacko came without whistling. He had caught their scent on the night breeze and stood by the fence, complacently waiting for his treat.

"I told you he was being spoiled," Marc said, leaning against the railing, watching her rub the horse's neck. "You'll ruin him for life."

"I don't believe it," she laughed, handing Jacko the remaining carrot. "This is lovely country, Marc. If I could get a job in town I'd buy a horse and board it so I could explore forever."

"You could keep her on our ranch," he offered.

She stared at him. Did he really mean that—did he really want her to stay nearby?

"You tempt me, Marc." She fought to keep her inflection light. She decided to change the subject. "Are you going down tomorrow with the first shift?" she asked.

"No, Ray is going, and we'll take off the following day with the calves. It takes a little over a day to get them to winter pasture."

They returned to the fire. Debra settled into her sleeping bag. Tomorrow would be the last night to admire the beauty of the stars in their black velvet backdrop.

She turned her head to look at the long form stretched next to her. The moon highlighted his tawny hair and strong shadows lay across his face. Her hands remembered the spring of his hair, as alive as the man. If only she dared to put out her hand and touch it!

Marc moved and his arm came out from the sleeping bag. His hand moved along her face in a gentle caress. A finger outlined the soft curve of her lips and she moved instinctively to kiss it as she met his eyes. His hand moved up to her forehead to push back a tendril of hair.

Her heart sang with joy. He wasn't immune to her! Was this what being in love was—to be so exquisitely attuned to every nuance that it could cause untold happiness or dejection? *Don't think beyond today, you silly goose,* she chastised herself. *You have known him only two weeks. You know so little about his private life. What if there's someone he's committed to?*

The thought chilled her and she thrust it aside. Resolutely, she let the memory of his caress take over, and the way his finger on her lips had become a shared kiss. She dropped off to sleep with that thought in mind.

The following day Ray, with half the men, took off with the reluctant cattle. She watched them go, feeling the excitement of the moment. What a job it must have been in the old days with those long cattle drives to market!

The dust settled and she turned to clean the kitchen, determined to leave it neat for Dusty.

There would be only four men. They had a light day and would be staying close to camp.

That morning she had seen Marc's light blue eyes following her and sensed the tentative question in their depths.

The men demanded a last song fest that night. Sam was there with his guitar.

"Sing that song you played for us the first night," he begged. "I've never heard it before but I can't get the tune out of my mind."

"I'll have to tell my brother you enjoyed it," Debra smiled. "He wrote the melody."

Again her husky alto gave the tune a haunting inflection.

> "Oh come, oh love of my life,
> Sing the song of the ages with me . . ."

She laid the guitar down at the last words, raising her head to meet the full power of Marc's eyes upon her. Did he know she sang that song to him alone?

The extra horses had been taken that morning. There was no reason to go to the corral, but this was her last night and a restlessness drove her out from the campfire.

She walked to the small grove of trees where she had first heard the bitter words exchanged by the brothers. Again she sat in the shadow of the tall pine tree, her chin resting on her drawn-up knees. Her ear became attuned to the night sounds: the faint rustling in the leaves, a disgruntled chirp from a bird huddling against the cold, and an owl resuming its interrupted calling.

A rolling pebble alerted her. "Do you usually turn

into a wood nymph and hide under a tree?" Marc asked as he settled next to her.

How foolish for her heart to race whenever he approached. "I'm saying goodbye to everything. I can't thank you enough for giving me this opportunity, Marc. I was born a city gal but never felt so happy as I have this week. I'm storing pictures in my mind to sort out during the long dismal winter months."

"Winter here has its own beauty," he reminded her.

"I'm sure, but I can't take advantage of your hospitality to find out."

He turned his head to her. "There is no reason why not. If you take a position nearby and you have your horse with us, I could show you places no one has seen since the Indians."

"Oh, Marc, how you tempt me!" she said with longing.

She wanted to pursue the subject but knew it was foolish. What she longed for and what her common sense warned her to expect were two different things. She had parlayed a day's visit into a wonderful vacation. But that would end when they left this bit of heaven tomorrow. Marc might follow his offer to show her more of his ranch, but that would take only a day or two, and then she'd be back in Denver. She gave a little sigh. Her secretarial job never looked less interesting.

Her thoughts went back to his proposition. Would it be possible to find a job near by and take him up on his offer? She shook her head in resignation and sought to glean more information about his ranch.

"I heard some of your men discuss sheep," she said. "Do you run them also?" The concept had surprised her. Sheepherders and cattlemen were notorious enemies—at least in her books!

"Yes," he answered. "I took a busman's holiday to New Zealand to see how they work their ranches. They frequently run cattle and sheep together. Sheep can survive on pastures that can't support cows. I thought I'd give it a try and have subsidized two Basques to run the sheep on land I couldn't use, plus some I leased from the government."

"Has it been successful?" she asked with interest.

"Yes, we're beginning to show a profit, which is what it is all about. I even got some die-hard ranchers now willing to try it."

His voice lifted with enthusiasm. "The sheep should be down to winter quarters now. I will have to show your the dogs at work."

"I'd love that! I've seen movies about their skill but to actually see it!" Her voice rang happily into the night. He peered at her a long moment as edges of moonlight filtered through the overhead branches. He rose suddenly and extended his hands, assisting her to rise.

"I'd like to show you something," he said quietly.

She glanced at him, wondering where he was taking her. His arm went around her waist, and she knew with resigned helplessness that she would go unresistingly wherever he wished to lead her.

The dry grasses made crunching sounds under their shoes as they walked across a small field. Before them was a larger copse of trees and they headed toward it.

Marc stopped before they entered the deeper shadows. He gazed skyward and Debra followed his look. The moon was obscured by a large cloud and she realized he was gauging the time for its re-emergence.

"I have been here often in the daytime when searching for cattle. There's a stream that runs through here and it's a pretty place." He drew her closer so she now faced him. Her hand rested on his heavy jacket as she tried to see his expression hidden in the shadow cast by his Stetson.

"Then last year on a night similar to this, I happened to come this way again." He seemed to be waiting for something and she remained silent, content to be held even this casually in his arms.

The field lightened as the cloud passed, and the moonlight tipped the sagebrush in silver. Marc took her hand and led her into the deeper shadows.

They did not go far. She heard the chattering of the stream as it rushed over the stones, and looked forward with anticipation. It must be lovely indeed to have struck Marc so forcefully.

The trees parted and Debra gave a little gasp of delight. Before her was a small opening, a little fairy glen. The moonlight bathed it in silvery highlights, and the bubbling brook filled the air with gay music.

"Oh, Marc!" she breathed, enchanted. It was a magic place. She stepped into the circle of moonlight and it was as if the magic touched her. Bewitched, she turned to Marc, and was surprised to see he had removed his hat. She met his piercing gaze with a feeling of abandonment.

Then he entered the magic circle, joining her, his gaze never wavering as he came to her. A glow seemed to surround him and she wondered fleetingly if she looked the same to him.

It seemed as if destined that she should be in his

arms, to have her lips crushed by his. It was as if this was what the magic glen had been created for.

His hand moved caressingly over her cheek to bury itself in her hair as his mouth moved sensuously over hers, parting willing lips. Then, as if resenting the obstruction, he unzipped their jackets so their bodies could press closer. She reveled in the new warmth, the heavy beat of his heart over hers even as a wild delirium took over her senses.

Impatient fingers unbuttoned her shirt and slid over tingling skin until her breast was cupped lovingly, urgently, in his strong hand. She could understand the need to touch, to possess. Her hands were buried in his hair and she deplored the impeding clothes, craving to caress him as he was her.

She was his, and she gloried in the knowledge. She needed to become part of him. Here, in this perfect woodland glen with the magic moonlight bathing them.

She arched against him, acknowledging the passion she had aroused in him. Here, now, she was begging, knowing she was beyond the point of turning back.

Then, as he strained her even closer, the moon slipped behind a cloud. A finger of cold wind buffeted them, causing her to shiver.

No! The silent cry welled up in her in despair as she raised her eyes in supplication to the moon. But it was hidden from sight, taking its special magic with it. They were mere mortals again, standing in a darkened glen.

A shudder ran through her and it was echoed in

Marc. He held her close, his face buried in her hair until their ragged breathing eased and the wild thunder of their hearts returned to normal.

Silently he buttoned her shirt and rezipped her jacket. Then, after a gentle kiss, tender with promise, he took her hand and led her away the way they had come.

Debra couldn't look back. The moon was still hidden, and she wanted to remember the little glen as it had been first seen, bathed in moonlight magic.

They joined the men for a last cigarette. When she turned to zip herself into her sleeping bag she caught Bill's glance. He gave her a slow knowing smile. Her cheeks flamed. She had spent the past half hour in Marc's arms. Were the stars still in her eyes for all to see? She hoped not.

Chapter Seven

Debra rode down in the truck with Marc while the rest herded the bewildered calves. Some were still searching for their mothers.

Dusty had a portable stove going and was waiting for them with a hot meal. A weather front had moved in and the day had been briskly cool.

"We'll have a few scattered warm days but they will be strictly bonuses," Marc said when Debra commented on the change. "One last night in the sleeping bag. I bet you're not sorry."

"I wouldn't have missed this week for anything," Debra said. "But I'm looking forward to a long hot bath! Right now I'm dreaming of wallowing in a tub full of heavenly bubble bath."

"Hm, yes. I'm getting the picture." Marc's gaze went slowly over her slim form before resting on her flaming cheeks. He burst into laughter. "Oh, Debra, what a mixture of opposites you are! One minute you're the innocent and the next you offer the world."

There was nothing she could say. He was well aware of her complete abandonment when in his arms. Fortunately, Dusty came over to report to Marc, saving her from having to frame a rejoinder.

"They got down without a mishap," he reported. And Ray sent some men to help at Pawson's. The cattle settled down fine in their new pasture. Also, the trucks will be coming the beginning of next week for the next batch to go to the market."

"Good," Marc said. "I'll set the men to cut out the ones to go. The market prices still holding firm?"

"Better. They're up some," Dusty said happily.

"It's about time. It will be nice to earn a profit to make up for the lean years," Marc said.

What a complex business ranching was! Did this man ever have time to relax? It seemed in a past age she had met the carefree man in the national park who confessed he was on a long-overdue vacation.

In the morning Marc waited until the men had the cattle started down on the last leg and then drove home.

"No need for us to play nursemaid today," he said as he avoided a pothole. "I'll get you to that hot bath. I admit the idea has been growing on me also. If you really want to wallow, you should try mine." He glanced at her. "You haven't seen my suite of rooms, have you?"

"I haven't even seen the kitchen," she reminded him. "We left before daybreak, remember."

A smile played on his lips. "I remember well. There was this wood nymph sitting in the dark.

. . . Then she turned those soft brown eyes sparkling with excitement—" He gave a deep sigh. "I have to do something about those eyes. Dark glasses, maybe."

He squinted down at her before the road reclaimed his attention. The rough lane made a sharp turn and the spread was laid out before them.

"Home," he said softly with a quiet pride. Her breath caught in her throat. *If only it were!*

He stopped in front of his house and stretched his arms. It had been a long hard drive keeping the truck from bouncing off the lane. "Joyce should be there now that Ray is back. Is Aunt Elsie enough of a chaperon or do we move you to their house?"

"My, are we proper now," she mocked teasingly. "No one would believe you slept next to me all this week! Please, Marc, I love my room overlooking your Fairy Falls. I would like to stay if it isn't too much bother. I'm here for such a short time it's senseless to move. Besides, if your sister-in-law has young twins on her hands, she won't appreciate an unannounced guest."

She watched as his grin softened his face. "I won't refute that argument because I'd like to keep you here. Besides, every evening when I telephoned down to Aunt Elsie, she was full of questions about you. She was afraid I was making you work too hard. I think she would like to have another woman around.

Aunt Elsie's face was wreathed in smiles as she hurried out to greet them. "You're back sooner than I expected! I've been keeping my eye out for the trail of dust from the cattle so I could gauge how long it would be before you arrived."

"How are you, dear?" she asked, turning to Debra. "None the worse for wear, I can see. It will take me no time to get lunch ready but I bet a bath is the first thing you want. I'm glad you're finally showing some sense, Marc, bringing her back so soon. You don't have to stand over the men all the time." She clucked happily around them, shooing them into the house. "Dusty can empty the truck. Go in and get presentable!"

Marc gave Debra a "See what I mean?" look and held the door for them.

Aunt Elsie bustled up with her and it was soon evident she was eager to find out how she had fared on the top corral.

Debra gave her a quick but carefully edited account of her days. "I loved every minute of it," she said happily. "I'm so glad you gave me the courage to sneak along!"

The older woman's eyes were bright buttons as she examined the young girl. "Ray said you were heaven sent. The food was excellent and you entertained them royally. You must play for me one of these days. But I'm holding you up, you poor dear! Get into that tub while I check lunch."

The bubble bath was all she had dreamed. She had spent the week in jeans and now decided on a pale green dress, giving into the desire to be feminine. The lines were simple and the soft material flowed smoothly along her slim firm curves. Her freshly shampooed hair shone with coppery highlights to cascade over her shoulders.

Marc's admiring glance as she came into the living room told her she had done the right thing. "It's too bad that ranch work seems to call for pants. I must say I like my women in skirts," he said rising to his feet.

His women. What did he mean by that? Really, the man was impossibly arrogant. She looked at him but he seemed serenely unaware that he had said anything untoward. He sat down again and continued to sort through a large pile of letters in front of him.

Debra made polite conversation with Aunt Elsie for a few minutes until he looked up and, tossing the mail back on the table in disgust, remarked, "I'll have to spend time with them later. I'm not letting anything get in the way of my promise to show you around. After lunch, why don't you change back into slacks; I have something I want you to see."

Debra's curiosity was whetted, but Marc refused to elaborate. Instead, they talked of other things throughout lunch.

"Wouldn't be surprised to find snow on the top of the mountain tomorrow," Marc observed. "We left just in time. I only hope it doesn't hit here."

"So soon?" asked Debra in surprise. "It just turned October."

"We've had blizzards in September," confirmed Aunt Elsie. "Don't forget, we're near Canada. The arctic winds can be chilling. Be sure to bundle up warmly when you go out this afternoon." She smiled at the girl.

Debra took Aunt Elsie at her word. When she came downstairs from changing after lunch she was wearing jeans and a warm sweater, and was carrying her quilted jacket. Marc took it from her and held it for her to put on. Together, they walked out into the cold.

"Where is your hat? And gloves? We will have to outfit you more warmly for our winters," said Marc. She was surprised to see the condensation in the air as he spoke. She rubbed her hands against the nipping cold before searching for her zippered pockets. A big tanned hand enclosed hers and kept it clasped as he drew it into his pocket.

"It's too sudden." she shivered against him. The warmth of his hand holding hers in his pocket was enough to send the tingling along her nerves.

They went by one barn and she saw a huge tractor inside with a complement of attachments. She spied Jacko in one corral with the horses that were brought down and expressed a wish to stop and pet him.

"Not now, Debra," he said. "You can take him a carrot later if you wish."

A filly in a smaller corral lifted soft inquisitive eyes as they approached. The sun glinted from the rich brown coat, strikingly similar to her hair coloring.

"Oh, Marc!" she exclaimed. "What a beauty!"

"You mentioned a horse the other day," he said. "I had just bought her and thought you'd be interested. It's yours if you want her."

Her face flushed with pleasure. She turned and flung her arms around him and planted a kiss on his chin.

"You can do better than that!" he exclaimed as he pulled her toward him to claim a proper kiss.

Her cheeks were rosy when he released her. She heard Dusty chuckling. "Now that's what I call being appreciative!"

Debra was too happy to be embarrassed and she climbed eagerly on the rail.

"Oh, Beauty, you darling thing," she called. "Come and say hello."

The filly lifted her head, then, with a soft whinny, she trotted over to greet the girl.

"Would you like to try her in a saddle?" Marc asked.

"Do you think she'll let me?" Debra cried eagerly.

Dusty brought out a beautifully worked saddle and fastened it while Marc saddled his powerful Shadow. He helped her up before mounting his magnificent horse, and she was again struck by how right they looked together. *A proud man on a proud horse,* she thought.

Dusty opened the gate and Marc led her to a trail along the lower slope of the mountain. When the terrain leveled off he urged his mount to a gallop and hers followed willingly enough. There could be no contest. Shadow was over a hand taller than the little filly.

He dismounted by a stream and watched critically as she came up.

"How does she handle?" he asked as he helped her down.

"Beautifully," she breathed happily. "You know you've trapped me, don't you, Marc. I have to see about working here now so I can be with her. How much is she? Can you wait a week before I pay you? I'll have to transfer from my savings to my checking account when I get back."

"She's not for sale," he said.

Debra stopped in consternation and stared at him. "But, Marc!" she cried, "you can't do that to me. That isn't fair. You knew I would want to buy her."

"But I've decided I'll keep her," he said coolly.

"That's cruel of you!" she stormed, anger forming red circles on her cheeks. "I've wanted her since I first saw her. Besides, who will ride her? She's too dainty to ride the range."

He lifted his shoulders in a light shrug. "We do have women guests you know."

She stared at him in horror. Beauty was not a horse to be subjected to haphazard treatment from a visitor. Her eyes were huge with dismay and a suspicious brightness came to them.

She saw the laughter growing in his eyes.

"Marc, you beast," she gasped, as relief flooded her. "You've been teasing me!"

He gathered her close and she could feel his chest rumble with laughter. "The lady has a temper." He pushed back his Stetson and lowered his head. She was lost again, unable to control her response.

"Ah, yes," he said thickly when he finally raised his head. Tenderly he pushed back a strand of hair before placing kisses on the corners of her mouth. "What am I going to do about you, young lady?" he whispered against her lips. "Do I let you get into my blood?"

What answer could she give? She wanted to hold him fiercely and let her lips, her body tell all. She lay like a quivering bird in the curve of his arm, her lashes lowered so he wouldn't see the yearning.

His finger went under her chin and her soft brown eyes were raised to meet the question in his. She moistened her lips with the tip of her tongue before giving him a timid smile.

"We'll have to wait and see what the future brings, won't we," she whispered.

He smiled into her eyes and cupped her face gently before kissing her.

I know what I want, her heart cried. *Oh, Marc, do you have any doubts? I'm yours already, irrevocably, can't you see? I'll wait, but don't take too long.*

He gathered the reins of the horse while looking at the lowering sky. "You know, I would have sworn the sun was shining! We'd better get back before this hits us."

"Do you have storms here like the one we had at the Park?" she asked as he helped her mount.

"Definitely. It's hard to forecast how severe they'll be because they hide behind the mountains and we can't see what is building up."

They returned at an easy canter and Debra insisted on rubbing Beauty down while he took care of his horse, then they went into the house.

She was taking a shower when it occurred to her that Marc had not quoted a price for Beauty. *I must remember to ask him,* she thought as she toweled herself dry. She wrapped the towel around her body to answer Aunt Elsie's knock.

Only it wasn't Aunt Elsie. Marc's tall frame filled the doorway. She heard the quick intake of his breath.

"I'm sorry, but you did say to come in." He leaned against the doorframe. "You look like a startled fawn. Relax, I'm not going to eat you. I had a brainstorm. We'll go out tonight for dinner and I wanted to tell you so you can dress for it."

She hesitated, clutching the slipping towel. "My wardrobe is limited. You've seen the extent of my evening clothes," she said. "Are we going to a fancy place?"

"You'll be perfect in any outfit," he assured her. He started to close the door, then poked his head back in the room. "The ankles were great, but the thighs are divine!" he said with a mischievous grin before shutting the door.

She gasped as she looked down. The towel had parted and the soft curve of one leg was exposed from the hip. It took awhile to reassure herself more was disclosed when wearing a bikini.

The clouds were still heavy with threatening rain when he escorted her to his car.

"A Jaguar, Marc!" she exclaimed. The low silvery car gleamed in the light from the window. She snuggled into the soft leather seat, enjoying the sensous sensation of the luxurious car. "I feel like purring," she laughed. "I could take to this good life very easily."

"You'd be easy to spoil," he agreed glancing at her, a smile curving his lips. "You think roughing it in a sleeping bag is a treat, and feeding a bunch of starving men a privilege. It's time for me to show you ranch life has its lighter side, also."

They were on the highway now and he reached for her hand. He placed it on his thigh with his hand clasped warmly over it. The muscles of his leg rippled whenever his foot manipulated the pedals, sending breathless impulses through her.

She was almost sorry when he turned into the parking lot in front of the restaurant.

Sitting at a small, semi-secluded table, Debra blamed the glow she was experiencing on the unaccustomed wine. She complimented the waiter on the food, but she had no idea what she was eating. She felt as though she and Marc were enclosed in their own private bubble that nothing could ever burst. She wanted to listen to his deep, resonant voice forever and drown in the warmth of his blue gaze.

"Marc! Darling! How wonderful to see you out of the hospital! Why didn't you call me?"

The woman standing beside their table was eye-catching, from her impeccably set hair to the soft white hands with their flaming red fingernails. Her low-cut, black satin gown outlined her generous curves.

Marc dropped Debra's hand on the table. Did she imagine that it was with a flicker of impatience? He rose politely. "Margo! I thought you were still in Europe—"

"You know that's next month," she pouted. "I hope you forgive me, lover, for not visiting you in the hospital. You know I can't stand those places; they make me ill."

Marc made the introductions. "Margo, this is my houseguest, Debra Wayfield."

Icy blue eyes glared at her before fluttering up to Marc.

"That's not fair, darling. You haven't even invited *me* to see that fabulous showcase of a house. You promised, you know! I'll drop by tomorrow since you're not keeping it to yourself anymore," she said sweetly.

"I won't be there," he said firmly. "Wait until later this month. I plan to throw a party then."

"You'd better include me!" Margo said. "It's

about time you showed it off! A fabulous house like that for a bachelor? At least you must let me hostess it. I know a perfect couple who cater beautifully."

"I'll keep your offer in mind," he said.

Debra gave a tight smile as they said their farewells. She sat with her hands clasped tightly in her lap as she watched Margo, hips swinging provocatively, walk across the room to join a party of friends at another table. *This pain tearing through me can't be jealousy,* she thought. *And it can't be love. Love is mutual trust. But there has been no declaration of love,* she reminded herself. Unable to sort out her confused emotions, she reached shakily for another glass of wine. Its coolness felt good sliding down her parched throat.

"Careful, girl, that isn't your water glass!" Marc admonished. Debra stared in surprise at the empty goblet. "I—I . . . you're right," she said in confusion.

His eyes narrowed. "I think I'd better order you some coffee."

Marc was dissolving into a golden mist by the time the coffee came and Debra was afraid to lift the cup.

"Marc, how much wine have I had?" she whispered, blinking eyes now wide as she tried to focus. Odd how difficult it was to enunciate properly! The words came out better if she spoke slowly.

His mouth was set in a hard line as he signaled for the check. He leaned forward and his broad shoulder formed a screen as he poured cream into the cup and lifted it to her lips.

"It's not too hot now. Chug-a-lug, Debra. I'll take you out in the fresh air to clear those mists from that silly head."

She drank the coffee dutifully. She could not have navigated to the door without the support of his arm around her waist. Her feet floated on a cloud. Vaguely, she noted the quick flash of Margo's eyes as they passed near her table.

He rolled down the windows of the car and tucked a robe around her before speeding into the darkness. The cold wind came as a shock and she shivered under the cover. After a few miles he stopped in a turnoff and put up the windows.

"Can't give you pneumonia," he said. "Feel any better?"

"I—I'm embrassed, I mean embarrassed," she said and started giggling. "I've never been ine-inebriated before."

"What an innocent you are! A little wine and you're flying." She could not see his expression in the dark, but his voice was mocking.

She turned and leaned forward to look up into his face. "I know what happens now," she said, nodding wisely. "According to the scr-script, the big seduction scene starts."

His eyes roved over her face. "No," he said firmly. "When you come to me I want you to remember every minute of it."

She nodded her head again at the sheer profundity of the statement. If only her eyes would focus better! She raised her hand to caress his cheek. "I would like that, Marcus," she murmured.

Nestling her head on his shoulder, she sighed contentedly. And fell asleep.

Chapter Eight

The first thing she saw was her blouse and long skirt folded carefully over the chair. She swung out of bed to close the window against the cold, and stared unbelievingly down at herself. She was in her lace bra and long half-slip.

I must have been in some state when Marc got me home, she gasped. *I don't even remember undressing this far. In fact I don't remember anything after Marc pulled the car to the turn-off. . . .*

She stopped, aghast. What happened after that? She recalled the meeting with Margo and the painful knot of jealousy that curled in her stomach. Then a delicious floating sensation. *But what else?* Surely she . . . surely Marc . . . !

She covered her burning cheeks with shaking hands as she concentrated fiercely, trying to remember. She hadn't a clue. She felt her lips. They held no trace of bruising pressure. Hadn't Marc at least kissed her? She was perversely annoyed. Had

. . . had Marc undressed her? She hurried into the shower to cool her fevered thoughts. She was now conscious of the pounding behind her eyes and an abnormal thirst. She took two aspirin and went downstairs, reluctant to unravel the embarrassing truth.

Marc had already started breakfast. Thank goodness Aunt Elsie wasn't there.

He watched with amusement as she thirstily drank the orange juice. "I didn't expect you up so soon after last night," he said as he poured coffee for her.

Her hand shook when lifting the cup and she quickly replaced it on the saucer. She swallowed hard. How did one ask a man how far he went the night before?

"Marc, er, about last night . . . ?" *Why did her voice have to quaver so?*

He raised an eyebrow in question. He wasn't going to make it easy for her, she could see.

"I—I hope I wasn't too objectionable last night." By his answer she would have an inkling of what had happened.

"Objectionable? My dear girl, last night you were far from that," he said. He looked sharply at her bent head. "Don't tell me you don't remember anything that happened?"

She shook her head in misery. This was worse than she feared. "I don't remember anything after you stopped the car," she whispered.

"I must be slipping. That's the first time a woman ever told me she remembered nothing. Yet you seemed to enjoy it, Debra. Or am I wrong?" He grinned wickedly.

She raised a face filled with anguish. The paper napkin became tatters in her hands.

"I apologize for not putting your nightgown on after carrying you to your room but I didn't want to stay too long in case Aunt Elsie woke up. You were clinging to me so! You can be quite insatiable with a little wine, you know. I'll have to remember that."

Debra turned white then red. If only there was an earthquake to swallow her! To have become alive with desire in his arms was one thing, to have succumbed without a memory was unthinkable. She managed to sit immobile while Sophia placed bacon and eggs before her and brought a fresh pot of coffee. Food! The thought nauseated her.

His hand went over hers when the kitchen door swung closed.

"Debra, look at me," he commanded.

Look at him! All she wanted to do was flee from the house, but her hand was imprisoned in his clasp.

"You shouldn't rise so quickly to the bait! It wasn't very nice of me, but you were so vulnerable, obviously expecting the worst."

Her breath caught in a sharp gasp as she realized he had been teasing. The flood of relief was quickly followed by a surge of fury. She struggled to pull her hand from his firm grasp.

"That was despicable, Marc!" she flared, her eyes shooting sparks of anger.

"Anger becomes you, Debra," he said teasingly. "But don't protest too much or you'll have me believing you regret nothing happened."

His words caught her up sharp. Was there a grain of truth to them? Her resentment slipped away beneath his mocking eyes. She giggled, "Don't ever do that to me again, Marc!" Now her hand was steady when she lifted the coffee cup. "Do you think you can tell me what really happened?

"Nothing, actually," he admitted. "You fell asleep on my shoulder and I carried you upstairs and took off your dress and shoes. You were out like a light. Unfortunately, there were no clinging arms."

He did not add how he had tenderly pulled the covers over her and placed a kiss on her lips.

The wind was cold and heavy with the threat of rain. Even so Debra insisted on riding the little filly, Beauty. She went off on a brisk gallop. Marc had to check with his men about which animals were to be ready for shipment.

The rain started immediately upon her return. Marc was already back, immersed in the neglected paperwork on his desk in his room.

She paused in the doorway to offer her assistance. "After all, I'm a secretary," she reminded him.

The phone rang, stopping his curt refusal and she knew from his guarded voice it must be Margo. She turned to leave, ignoring his hand motioning her to remain. She'd give him the opportunity to talk freely.

Aunt Elsie had lit the fireplace in the living room and she sank gratefully on the thick rug in front of it. The woman was busy knitting a bulky sweater that was a shade darker than Marc's eyes. She shook herself with annoyance. Did everything have to be judged in relationship to this man?

Her heart gave the answer. Everything. Forever.

She bowed her head from Aunt Elsie's quick birdlike glances. What was she going to do about the tight knot that again burned in her following that telephone call? Was he going out with Margo tonight? It was obviously time for her to leave. While Aunt Elsie couldn't be more warm and friendly, there was building in her a frightening urgency to be near this forceful man, to wait achingly for his next kiss.

He was too vibrantly male. He would soon stop being satisfied with kisses. She trembled, wondering how strong her resistance would then be.

It was not in her to be a playmate. She wanted more with this man, but those searching blue eyes gave nothing away of his private thoughts.

Marc tossed a cushion to her and, grabbing another, sank to the floor beside her. He stretched out in front of the fire and watched the sheets of water run down the expanse of glass.

"Thank God this storm waited until we finished up there," he said fervently.

"I can imagine what the ground is like now," Debra shuddered while settling against the pillow. "Where would we have slept?"

"In the mess hall, naturally," he answered. "We've had to pack in there several times but we all agreed we liked to be outside whenever possible. I offered to build a bunkhouse even though we would only use it during roundup, but was vetoed. The youngsters like to believe they're living the life of the old West, and the old-timers refuse to admit it's hard on their bones."

"And most of all the stars are closer and the outdoors smells so good," Debra murmured sleepily. The heat from the fire was placing drowsy fingers on her eyes. Maybe she would find time for a nap after lunch.

"I called Ray to find out if Joyce and the monsters were back," Marc said to Aunt Elsie. "She arrived this morning and we're invited over after dinner. She's anxious to meet the new camp cook." He gave Debra his lopsided grin that put a triphammer to her pulse.

For dinner that night Debra changed into a cream-colored wool dress. She fastened a gold chain belt around her slim waist and selected heavy gold hoop earrings. Her hair was brushed into the soft loose flip she knew Marc preferred. She eyed herself critically in the full-length mirror. Smart as well as warm. Debra always dressed with a flair but until now it had been for her own enjoyment. Now she was dressing for the man she loved. It was a new experience to know one man's approval held so much power over her.

Debra had no preconceived idea what Joyce would look like but she was still a surprise. She was even taller than she—practically six feet and model thin. Her dark hair was fashionably streaked and worn in a carefully careless windblown effect.

She greeted Debra with an infectious grin. "I don't believe it!" she cried with a warm laugh. "Ray said you were a dream cook and easy to look at, but I had visions of a plump *hausfrau* type with a mothering complex!"

Two small tornadoes hurled themselves at Marc. They were encased in bright blue flannel nightclothes and emitted shrieks of delight. Marc collapsed on the floor from their onslaught and the three became part of a wrestling match.

"Come to the fire, Debra," she said with a tolerant smile. "We might as well leave them until they sort themselves out. This happens every time they haven't seen him for twenty-four hours. Don't get them too worked up, Marc, or you have to sit on them until they go to sleep," she called over the squeals.

Ray greeted her with a hug, then held her away. "You looked pretty good to us up there, but in a dress you're a knockout!" he said effusively.

Marc firmly extricated himself from the clinging bodies and came into the living room carrying a giggling boy under each arm. His hair was rumpled from his frolic and his face flushed, but even disheveled, he caused her heart to pound.

"You haven't been properly introduced to the nephews," he said. "Monster One is David and Monster Two is Bryan."

The boys waved from their awkward positions. Bright mischievous faces grinned at her and she saw they were identical twins, little replicas of their father.

"As long as you have them under control, whisk them to bed, will you, Marc?" Joyce asked. "Maybe they'll behave for a change and go to sleep without too much trouble." She raised her shoulders in a shrug as if that hope was slim, and followed the giggling boys still clamped under their uncle's arms.

Ray settled in a comfortable leather chair across from her. "How do you like the mare Marc brought?" he asked.

Debra smiled happily. "I love her dearly and she rides beautifully."

"I hope this rain passes quickly so you can get some long rides on her," Ray said. "We have some good trails and wonderful scenery here." His voice held a bitter note and Debra eyed him questioningly. His face was somber as he stared into his glass. Tight lines bracketed his mouth, but he offered no explanation.

Though the evening passed pleasantly enough, Debra could sense an undertow of tension. She could not understand it. Marc was obviously fond of his brother and his family, and they appeared to return his affection. Nevertheless, when Marc lifted an eyebrow at Debra, and suggested that it was time for them to go home, she could not help feeling a certain relief.

"Time for this rancher to go to bed," Marc said, his tall frame hovering by the door.

"But Marc, we haven't yet heard your decision," Joyce protested. Ray was frowning.

Marc stiffened. "There is no decision as far as I'm concerned!" All warmth disappeared from his face.

"Except for using this place, we have no intention of letting anyone wander around this side of the mountain," she persisted.

"How are you going to get your people from here to the other side without trespassing by my house?" Marc said scathingly. "The only natural trail to get to your playland runs smack in front of it. I'll be damned if I'll move or rebuild someplace else. You know even as a kid I said that was where my house would eventually go, and there it stays!"

Ray and Joyce exchanged bleak looks. This

charming old house was to be one of their drawing cards to give the authentic western atmosphere they were striving for! They needed access to it.

Marc held Debra's coat for her and she eyed the two men glaring at each other.

The farewells were far less friendly than the earlier greetings. "I'm sorry, Debbie," Joyce murmured to Debra, giving her a hopeless shrug. "The awful thing is we understand Marc's position but he won't see ours. There must be some middle ground where we can meet."

She scooped up the pile of ledgers and pressed them into Debra's arms. "Here, take them. If they get to his house maybe he will at least look at them."

They were the last thing she wanted but, unless she dropped them on the floor, she had to walk out of the house with them.

Marc made no effort to take them as they dashed through the rain to his car. Darn it, how did she get involved in this family feud?

When they reached his house he pointed to his room and told her to put them on his desk, as if even touching them was more than he could tolerate. There had been no conversation on the short run between houses. Marc was still angry and Debra held her counsel. He would open to her if and when he wanted to talk.

Marc hung her wet coat by the kitchen door with his. "Would you like another drink, or perhaps some coffee?" His words, his whole stance, were politely aloof. How could he make her feel so alone even with him in the same room?

"A cup of hot chocolate would taste nice on a night like this. Would you care to join me in one?"

she asked, resentful that she was getting the backlash from the quarrel between the brothers. There was too short a time left to her visit to have any part of it spoiled like this.

"I haven't had any since I was a child. Yes, I'll join you," he said, suddenly amenable as he sank into a chair by the table.

They took the mugs of hot chocolate to the living room. Marc added a log to the still-glowing embers in the fireplace and they sat before it without turning on the lights.

Slowly she drew him out, asking questions about his cattle and stating she would love to see the loading.

The log crumbled and he rose to push back the scattered embers. It was getting late and she went to gather the mugs. Marc's arms went around her and he held her gently against his lean body as he laid a cheek on her hair.

"Oh, Debra," he said, "am I so wrong in wanting to preserve this ranch from the trampling of strangers? They talk as if they could control them but you know how curious people are. I can just see them climbing fences and getting mixed in with the bulls, and, even worse, peering in my windows.

"I can't give this ranch up. It meant everything to Dad, and it's my life blood. I can't imagine starting out all over again someplace else, and that's what I'd be driven to do if I agreed to their scheme. I'm not gregarious like Ray and couldn't stand the noise of crowds so close. I realize ranch life isn't his thing. Perhaps with what Uncle Roger and I can scrape up between us, they can buy another place."

He sighed and rubbed his cheek along her silken

hair. She stood still in his arms, her hands clasped around his waist, happy she could offer him this outlet for his pain. He was trying to better understand his brother's dream even if diametrically opposed to his.

"You'll come up with a solution," she whispered against his shoulder. She saw the muscle jumping along his jaw and on impulse, leaned forward to place a soft kiss on it. "Don't fret anymore tonight."

His lips came down on hers, and when he finally held her away, his voice was husky. "For your information, you do alarming things to my blood pressure. Be gone, woman. I'll see you in the morning." His pressure was firm as he pushed her to the stairs.

The sun was shining when Debra arose in the morning, but it was bitingly cold. An edging of ice glinted around the puddles. She joined Aunt Elsie in the kitchen and sat at the table with a welcomed cup of coffee.

"If I were to stay any longer I'd be forced to buy warmer clothes," she said. "My wardrobe is fine for city living but not for this."

"I'll have to take you into town to get what you need," Marc said, coming in.

"Don't tell me you have been working already!" Debra said, seeing his face reddened from the cold.

"Ranchers can't afford to be sleepyheads." He laughed as he placed an icy hand along her warm neck.

She gave a shriek and Aunt Elsie clucked reprovingly.

"That's not a nice thing to do, Marc," she said,

bustling to hurry his breakfast. "Pour the poor man some coffee, Debra. He's finished quicker than usual."

Marc wrapped his hands gratefully around the steaming cup. "The men have things well under control. No one wastes time in this weather. It's easier to get the work done in a hurry."

Dusty drove up in the truck and brought in the stack of mail. Marc put the journals to one side and opened the letters, then sighed.

"I should get these out today. Things have backed up more than I anticipated."

"Then let's get to them," Debra said with alacrity. "And no argument. Is it too cold to ride Beauty today?"

"It should be bearable after lunch," he said. "Come on, slave driver, you've convinced me; we'll tackle these now."

Debra saw the pile of ledgers was untouched, but she didn't dare to say a thing as she settled down to the typewriter. Soon they even made a dent in some of the old correspondence and Marc smiled, satisfied with the accomplishment as they went to saddle the horses.

"I definitely will get a part-time secretary now that I see how much easier it is to have help. Care to apply?"

"What do I do with the rest of my time?" she asked over the catch in her throat. "You only need a cook during roundup time."

"Oh, I dare say we'll think of other uses for you," he said casually. "You'd be able to ride Beauty every day and Aunt Elsie could spoil you. And we could get together occasionally . . . How does the package deal sound?"

"Tempting," she laughed, keeping it light. "You know my weakness about being on a ranch, but what would your friends say if you kept a built-in secretary?"

"They would only be jealous!" He chuckled.

You're getting the right idea, she gloated, *but I'm not accepting those terms. I couldn't last seeing, wanting you every day and having no guarantee for the future. It's all or nothing for me.*

The road swept closer to the tall stand of timber, almost overwhelming them as it soared toward the sky. "What is the name of the mountain?" she asked, intent on changing the subject.

"Reede," he answered. "Reede Mountain. What else could it be? It's not tall as mountains go, but it's ours."

"I'm impressed. I've never met a person who had a mountain named for him."

"Not me," he corrected. "The family."

"Perhaps, but you are part of the mountain and it knows you're its keeper," she murmured as if to herself.

She did not see his quick appraising glance.

The road rounded a hillock and she pointed to a stream. "Does that come from your mountain?"

"Yes, that draws from the lake," he said.

"Then if we followed it, we'd get to the west side?" she asked. She was hearing so much about this other side and was frankly curious to see it. "Would it be difficult?"

"No, there are a few rapids, naturally, coming

down from that height. There's a trail of sorts that fishermen use to get to the lake."

"Then you let people go there?" she asked in surprise.

"Of course. The local people have free access to it, though if Ray and Joyce have their way I guess it would become off-limits." The tightness was back in his voice and Debra was annoyed over inadvertently introducing that sore subject.

He turned Shadow onto the trail. They started climbing and Debra realized they were on the west side of the mountain. She looked around curiously. It was more rugged. Tall pines and clumps of aspen clung in pockets halfway up the side. Sagebrush softened bare rock.

"This is the other end of the stream," Marc informed her as he pulled in the horse.

The small lake spread before them in blue splendor, reflecting the clear sky. An island of trees stood in its center. What a gem to have tucked away here! The traitorous thought flashed through her that she could understand Ray's desire to show it off to the world. What an ideal setting for a lodge! The water no doubt would be warm enough in the summer for swimming and she could envision small sailboats skimming its surface. When frozen in the winter, the iceskating would be perfect.

She leaned forward in the saddle and pointed. "Marc don't tell me you're blessed with two Fairy Falls!"

A long plume of water cascaded over a cliff not too far away. Debra was aware that the noise, while muted by distance had been clamoring to be identified.

"That one is named Roger's Falls. My uncle was the first to discover it when they homesteaded. Come, I'll take you to it."

They turned the horses and the sound soon became a muffled roar as they climbed, picking their way carefully around the boulders.

It was a miniature Firehole Canyon. Now she knew what Marc was referring to that time they were looking into the chasm at Yellowstone.

"It's beautiful!" she cried, raising her voice above the noise of the falling water. She looked up to where it started and saw the rainbow shimmering in the mist.

He let her drink her fill of the scenery, then turned back onto the trail. When they could again talk without shouting, he pulled up his horse.

"How lucky you are to have all this beauty tucked away here!" Debra sighed. "Too bad your houses aren't closer so you could admire it all every day."

"Now that you have seen it, do you understand why I don't want it trampled over and changed?" he demanded.

Debra hesitated. Why did she always understand and sympathize with both sides of an argument? Marc was right, yet Ray had his dreams, also. Who was right, and who was wrong? There were too many imponderables.

"I see you are not with me in this question!" Marc's voice whipped out at her and she looked at him, startled at its intensity. His eyes were hidden in a squint against the sun, but his mouth was a taut line. Debra shivered at the cold anger on his face.

She put her hand out in protest, but he had moved Shadow ahead on the trail. His wide shoulders formed a rigid fence that filled her with despair. How did she get tangled in the controversy? Both sides seemed intent on using her as a sounding board. She was an outsider and shouldn't be placed in this awkward position. She resolutely held back the tears of frustration. Marc had become a flaming need but his icy silence was turning any shared fire into cold ashes.

He didn't speak to her on the trip back. Nor did he stop to point out any special sights.

Anger grew inside her. She had done nothing to deserve this treatment. If he was so unmovable in his convictions and had spurned her because he thought she was against him, she'd better cut connections now before she was hopelessly involved in what could become a bitter stalemate.

She glared balefully at his back. As soon as she could speak to him alone, she would tell him she was leaving. It wasn't good for a guest to stay this long. His show of annoyance indicated he was becoming tired of her. His kisses resulted only from a man—woman chemistry he'd feel with any presentable woman with whom he was forced into close proximity. She was crazy if her dreams hoped for more. His expertise clearly showed he had held others in his embrace, even . . . Margo.

She had been resolutely trying to keep that woman from her thoughts but it was impossible. Margo had been in Marc's arms. She was certain. Her behavior was clear proof. Again the knife of jealousy stabbed her.

Darn you, Marcus Reede, she raged silently at his back. *I was perfectly happy before you came into my life. And I will be happy again. But not until I have left you and Reede Mountain for good.*

By dinnertime Marc had gotten over his anger. He could even discuss his brother's plans dispassionately, and told Aunt Elsie about the ledgers foisted on Debra.

"I would like to see them," she said. "I told them I would lend some money also, but only if all of you first reached an amicable agreement.

A shaft of annoyance lit Marc's eyes but he was determined to keep the evening pleasant.

The plump woman retired early, murmuring something about a book she was engrossed in.

"Come here," he said softly. She met his eyes and her heart started pounding. His hands caught her wrists and she tumbled into his lap.

He cradled her head on his shoulder as one hand gently stroked her hair. Soft kisses ran along the silken edge. "Why are my arms so empty when you aren't in them?" he murmured.

All her frustrations melted away. She snuggled against him, thrilling to his nearness. The beating of his heart vibrated through the soft knit of his shirt and she placed her hand there as if to capture its power. The firelight flickered over them. They talked softly, telling each other their dreams while time stood still.

The log settled with a shower of sparks and they were silent, content to be in each other's arms as the room darkened. His arms tightened and her head tilted to meet his mouth. The kiss was a tender exchange but her lips clung when he started to lift his head. With a groan he crushed her tight, tenderness

165

giving way to passion. His warm hands cupped her breasts, now hard with desire. She slid her fingers under the knit shirt to caress the broad expanse of his chest.

His touch lingered along her thighs, consuming her with desire.

As in a feverish dream, she moved with him to his bedroom. His every touch became a promise. Their lips clung as his fingers found the fastening on her dress. A thrill shot through her when she felt her breasts crushed against his bare chest. She could feel the rough weave of the bedspread against her body and the heavenly weight of his body next to hers. She strained against him, her hands kneading the hard muscles of his shoulders.

"Debra, do you know what you're doing?" he murmured against her mouth.

Her arms tightened around his neck. There was no going back. "Don't leave me like this, Marc," she pleaded.

A spasm shuddered through him as he reclaimed her lips.

Knuckles rapped softly on his door. "Marc, are you still awake?" Aunt Elsie called in a whisper.

Marc buried his face in the pillow, giving a muffled oath.

He groped for his bathrobe and went to the door. He stood in the opening, carefully blocking any view into the room.

"Something wrong?" he asked.

"I was thinking about our conversation and decided to get those plans your brother talked about."

Marc digested the words for a moment. "There's quite a stack. I'll gather them and bring them up to your room."

"If it's no trouble," she said agreeably.

Marc closed the door and turned to see Debra struggling into her dress. His face was grim. He went swiftly to her side and clasped her shoulders. Their eyes met, his searching and hers dark pools in which the fires were slowly receding.

"What can I say, Debra!" he cried as he gathered her close.

She pushed him away gently. "Your aunt is waiting," she said composedly. But her fingers trembled, belying the surface calm as she smoothed her dress. He smiled ruefully as he closed the zipper up the back for her.

"Wait until I'm upstairs and can keep her occupied, then you can slip to your room." He stopped short and stared at her. "Hell, I'm acting like a damn conspirator in my own house," he said angrily. His hand went to her cheek. "There's so much to say . . ."

Her smile was tremulous. "Go upstairs," she urged.

His mouth had an angry set, and his kiss was hard and punishing. He gathered the books and strode out. She waited until he was up the stairs before following. She gave one last glance at the huge rumpled bed and marveled that legs so unwilling could carry her to her room.

Once there, she undressed as quickly as possible and got into bed. But she spent a restless night. She tossed and turned, feeling again Marc's gentle hands on her body, his mouth probing hers. Supposing Aunt Elsie had not interrupted them? She felt hot all over. It must not happen again. She would turn away from the demands she saw in his blue eyes, the promise she read in his lips. Finally she drifted into an uneasy sleep.

Chapter Nine

The day was exhilaratingly brisk and Beauty whinnied happily as she turned her down the long driveway. The truckers had called the day before to say they would come earlier than expected. She saw two huge trailors sitting a distance away, almost obscured by the dust as the cattle were cajoled into the narrow run that forced them up the ramp and into the vans. No more long dusty treks to market which had seemed so romantic in the stories she read. The trailer trucks came to the ranch to be quickly loaded and the cattle were sped to either the fattening farms or slaughter houses.

Marc was there supervising. This was big business and he was in full control of every aspect of it.

The bawling from the nervous cattle came wafting on the breeze and she felt a momentary sadness for them.

A rancher's wife would not misplace sympathy like this, she admonished herself sternly. Her heart lurched. A rancher's wife . . . Last night she had been perilously close to feeling like one. Her face flamed. But it would not happen again. She would never be "just one of Marc's women!" She would be his wife . . . or . . . nothing.

Her expression was determined as she chose the route alongside the road. The farms lay golden before her. The last of the hay was being bundled by the huge machines, spewing them out in neat rows. Would Marc have to buy hay this year? He had told her that he could grow enough himself unless winter was unusually long and harsh with a continuous blanket of snow. Always Marc! She must remove her thoughts from this big man and his ranch.

A rush of water alerted her to a stream ahead. This must be the trail leading to that gem of a lake. Reede Lake and Roger's Falls! Everywhere reminders of those tall, rangy men who had battled with and conquered the land! On impulse, she turned onto the faint trail that wound beside the stream. Was this called Reede's Brook? She had forgotten to ask. How wonderful to have all this and even a mountain to carry on one's name! Yet Debra could appreciate the responsibility it also carried. It sat more heavily on Marc's shoulders than on his brother's.

Too bad something so lovely was responsible for the tension between the brothers. Each was holding tight to his dream. She was a firm believer every problem had a solution, and she turned Beauty homeward, a frown marring her brow.

She found Aunt Elsie in the living room surrounded by the plans and open ledgers.

"What do you think of Ray's dream?" Aunt Elsie asked as Debra paused by the threshold.

Debra hesitated, still shying away from being drawn into this family controversy. Her heart was with Marc, but her head admitted both sides had valid arguments. "If there was only some way of moving the homestead next to Reede Lake, everything Ray wants would be on the west side. Then Marc would have his privacy. I don't believe he is against the resort idea, is he? It's the invasion of his property he's fighting."

"That's true," the woman admitted. A thoughtful look came to her face. "You may have come up with the answer. We were sitting so close to the problem, we couldn't see the obvious."

Marc came in, rubbing his hands against the cold. He ignored the papers on the coffee table and went to change. By common consent, the ledgers and plans were put away.

Sophia appeared at the door to tell Marc he was wanted on the phone. "It is that Miss Blair," she said, not hiding the note of displeasure.

Aunt Elsie's birdlike glance took in the quick tightening of Debra's lips. "Marc was dating Margo when he started building this house." she said. "We thought he might have had her in mind as its mistress, but I suspect it was more her wishful thinking than anything else. She had all their friends thinking the same. When he was off somewhere on the ranch, she used to sneak here while it was being built to take measurements, saying it was to surprise Marc. I used to think it very odd but kept my peace. Marc has never brought a woman here."

Debra flushed. "Oh, dear, he must have been resentful about inviting me here. I remember Miss Blair saying she hadn't been invited to see the house.

171

He said something about having a party sometime this month."

Aunt Elsie's busy fingers stopped their knitting as she looked up in surprise. "Well! That would be nice. The boys always had company at the other place and I could never understand Marc's attitude about this house. It was as if he were waiting for something to happen. He's had his cronies over but never one of his dates. That's why I was so surprised when you first came." She hurriedly picked up her knitting.

Debra stared at her tightly folded hands, trying to sort out what she had just heard. But more important was what Marc was saying to Margo. Was he trying to find time to have a date while she was still here? She was sure Aunt Elsie could hear the heavy thud of her heartbeat.

Marc returned to settle in his chair. "That was Margo," he said unnecessarily. "She reminded me that I had promised to have a party and again offered to hostess it. I assured her I had two very efficient women here who would do an excellent job."

He shifted to look at Debra. "I've been thinking next weekend would be a good time. It would be an ideal way to introduce you to the neighbors." A light glinted in the blue eyes. "The word is out that I'm harboring a beautiful woman here. My men must be spreading the word about your mighty hunting ability and the way you cook, not to mention your singing."

"Please," Debra protested with embarrassment. "You make me sound like some sort of paragon!"

"You sound like perfect material for a rancher's wife," Aunt Elsie said.

"I agree" Marc said smoothly. "That's why I'm giving the party. I have to introduce her around. We'll invite the eligible bachelors."

"That isn't necessary," Debra said stiffly. "I'm not looking for a husband." *Not looking. I've found whom I want.*

"Stop teasing the girl," his aunt said, gathering her knitting. "I'm going to make coffee before we go to bed. Is there anything else you would like?"

Marc put in a request for another sample of Sophia's sponge cake and Debra went to help carry the tray.

"I'm happy to hear Marc is finally entertaining," she said, handing Debra napkins and cups. "He has created such a lovely home and has never shown it off. Take that pad and pen along, dear. We may as well find out whom he wants to invite."

The list lengthened. "Marc," his aunt protested, "wouldn't it be better to cut this in half and have two parties? This is fast becoming a mob scene. No one will be able to appreciate the beauty of the house if they're packed in like sardines."

He laughed. "I got carried away." He took the pen and drew firm lines through half the number. "There, is that more manageable?" he asked, handing it back.

She nodded. "I'm going to have to press you into service, Debra. I'll need your help addressing the envelopes if we're to get them out tomorrow."

Chapter Ten

Debra stacked the envelopes in neat piles, then gave a sigh as she flexed her fingers. Thirty couples! She would have to buy a new dress. She couldn't let Marc down by appearing in what she had brought with her. A trip to town was imperative.

She went over the list again and gave a smile of pleasure. The one that had pleased her most was "Miss Margo Blair and Guest." Marc was not planning on being her escort.

"That looks like a smile of satisfaction," Marc said as he strode into his room carrying the day's mail. "Seeing that pile of envelopes, I can understand Aunt Elsie's reaction to the original list. I'll have to show you off to the rest of my friends another time."

Debra blinked as she harnessed her soaring heart. Where would she be after next week's party? The original overnight invitation was stretching into a month's vacation. Was he assuming she would work nearby so she could ride Beauty? Did he really want her to stay close by?

Please, her heart prayed. *Please make it so.*

She busied herself placing stamps on the envelopes before her. She had been extolled as a very efficient secretary, completely unflappable in emergencies. Why then did her emotions explode in all directions when this man was near! Surely she was adult enough not to collapse into adolescent dreams! She tried not to think of the kisses that had rendered her completely helpless to his will.

"Is the glue on those stamps so bad you have to pound them on?" Marc asked. "Or is there a private demon after you?"

Debra's head snapped up to meet the blue eyes laughing at her. He was leaning back in his chair, relaxed and somehow younger looking.

She gave him a puckish grin. "Don't we all have little demons chasing us at times? I just pounded mine to death."

His eyes lingered over her. "Good. I trust you'll have no more. The mail is light today and I don't feel like laboring over it. Come, we'll get the horses and go for a ride. The air is brisk but the wind is down so the chill factor is tolerable."

Debra hesitated. "Shouldn't I be helping Aunt Elsie?"

He shook his head. "I just left the kitchen. She and Sophia have everything planned and are now busy on the phone ordering. If you're through with those things, I'll give them to Dusty to mail."

Suddenly everything took on a holiday glow. The horses were eager for exercise. The air was sparkling clear, and while their breath condensed in small puffs, there was no stinging wind. Marc urged the horses to another section of the ranch that she had not as yet explored. The silos loomed large before them as he leaned over to open a gate. The cattle were more concentrated here and Debra realized this was where the cattle were fattened for market.

"I have to check on the feed for a minute, then we'll have our run."

As they headed home, the shadows were turning the purplish blue so typical of dusk in these mountains. Debra marveled as she watched them.

"Oh, Marc, do you think that I will ever see everything! Every day there is a new miracle!" Her soft, brown eyes were warm with delight.

"It takes a lifetime," he agreed. You have to see it in every season, under every weather condition. I still stop and admire a view and wonder why I had not noticed it quite that way before. Wait till you see us under fifteen-foot drifts of snow!"

"You will have to invite me again," she said, over the beat of her heart. Would she ever see this wonderful land in all its many moods? And more important to her, would she ever again see this tall man sitting easily in the saddle by her side? Involuntarily she sighed.

Since that night that had ended so abruptly in his room, Marc had been pleasant when they were together, but there had been no repeat of the soul-stirring performance of that eventful evening, no words of affection, not even a touching of hands.

Debra took her cue from him, hiding her hurt. Had he been able to push the flame of that night out of his mind, or more important, been repulsed by her easy capitulation?

Drat the man. He had her fluctuating like a yo-yo. One minute high with memories, the next in black dejection.

She would have to take it one day at a time, hoping the gods would finally smile upon her.

They circled back on a different route that ended at the driveway. They chatted companionably as they trotted past his brother's house on the way to the stable. A station wagon was in front of the house. Debra read the neat lettering on the door. LARSEN AND DIXON, ARCHITECTS. She saw Marc stiffen. All warmth had left his face and his eyes turned to blue ice.

Oh, no! She descried the change that came over him. The easy camaraderie disappeared as the horses went eagerly to their stalls.

He excused himself, saying he had to check some matter with Dusty, and Debra returned unhappily to the house.

As Debra passed by the living room she saw Aunt Elsie, papers and ledgers in front of her, sitting on the sofa talking to a strange man. Their voices were hushed. As Aunt Elsie appeared not to notice her, Debra decided not to stop. After all, these were family matters and did not concern her.

Later, from her room, she could hear the angry rumbling of Marc's voice interspersed by Aunt Elsie's birdlike twittering. She decided not to emerge from her room until she heard the architect's car pull out.

"Well, child," Aunt Elsie said, when Debra

appeared dressed for dinner in her long, green plaid skirt and scoop-necked green shell blouse, "we could have used your ideas this afternoon."

Marc did not appear to hear Aunt Elsie, or at any rate made no response. He was angrily pacing the room, his back to them. She ached to be by his side, to hold his hand, to comfort him, but instead she sat down by Aunt Elsie.

Aunt Elsie passed the plans over to her. "We've been trying to shift the position of the road from the homestead, but the only feasible place for it is still in front of here." Aunt Elsie shook her head regretfully, then let her gaze wander over to Marc who had stopped his pacing to stare at her angrily.

"In no way am I going to have a thoroughway by my house!" he shouted angrily.

Debra leaned forward. "Marc," she said. "I have an idea. Today I rode in from the highway trail next to the creek emptying from Reede Lake. Surely, it would be no more difficult building an entrance from there than through here!" The solution had been building in her as she studied the plans.

"And the lodge!" Aunt Elsie interrupted, caught up with the idea. "The obvious plan is by the lake! Of course! How obtuse of us not to see the answer under our very noses! Marc, surely you can have no objections now!"

Reluctantly, Marc came over to sit on the chair next to the sofa. "You just may have the solution," he admitted. "Let me sleep on it."

The next morning Marc made no mention of the evening's debate. "We have to round up a few more cattle and then the afternoon is yours," he informed Debra.

She begged to go with him and Marc gave into her pleading, providing she rode Jacko.

"Beauty isn't a trained range horse," he explained, seeing her crestfallen face. "I don't want to be worrying about the two of you."

Under his firm orders, she rode on the outskirts but still managed to turn in some bolting cattle and herd them back. She rode over to Marc, wildly excited over her first actual mustering, eyes shining, face lit with the thrill. Her childhood dream had finally come true!

"How about hiring me, boss man!" she exclaimed. Marc laughed into her eyes at her delight, and the world was so beautiful she thought her heart would burst from her joy.

"Had enough riding?" he asked as they rode back. "It's not too cold. We can take Beauty for a short ride after lunch if you wish."

"I heard her whinnying. She's expecting us." Debra agreed happily, still riding high from excitement.

His eyes burned over her and he pulled her close for a hard rough kiss, ignoring the grinning cowboys.

Oh wonderful day, oh wonderful ranch, oh wonderful man!

Aunt Elsie was out. She had gone into town, Sophia informed them as she served lunch.

Marc was claiming her attention. Suddenly every look, every gesture, every touch was telling her of his love. Surely tonight, when they were alone, she would hear the words.

Even the act of saddling their horses was a love song, singing between them. His lips feathered along

179

her cheek as he helped her up. Never had a day held such beauty.

They turned onto a trail along the lower reaches of the mountain to make a wide swing toward Reede Lake.

He pulled ahead when the trail narrowed and her vision was full of the man riding tall in the saddle.

She spurred Beauty on to draw closer when Marc pulled up suddenly. Shadow reared protestingly on his hind legs. With a sharp oath, he jumped off the horse and bent over something on the trail.

Debra slid off her mount to hurry over to see what had caused such consternation. There, waving brightly on a marking stick, was a small red flag.

Chapter Eleven

Marc stood up to look down the trail. A line of bright red dots marched ahead to disappear around a blocking boulder.

"Survey flags?" she questioned.

"They weren't here two days ago," he exploded, his voice quivering with rage. "This is Ray's doing. All that sweet talk about looking for a working agreement didn't amount to a hill of beans," he continued bitterly. "So this is his way of throwing down the gauntlet. He can't tell it to my face!"

Debra stared at him helplessly, wondering how to assuage his anger.

He stalked back to the big horse and Debra reached out a restraining hand. "Wait, Marc," she cried hopefully. "There must be an explanation for this! Ray wouldn't go behind your back."

He turned a frozen mask to glare icily at her. "Of course not," he said bitterly. "Those red flags just walked that nice straight line and planted themselves. They will also build that nice straight road in front of my house all by their little selves.

"Whose side are you on anyway?" he flared. "Are you planning to ski down those slopes already? Maybe you can set up a concession outside my house and show the points of interest viewed through my conveniently placed windows. As an added attraction I might even add local color for you and wear a sequined cowboy outfit in my living room!"

Debra drew back as if whipped. Anger welled up at the cruel accusations.

"What a charming idea!" she stormed. "I would never have thought of that by myself. And just think, the summer guests can have cooling dips in the pool under your Fairy Falls!"

For a horrible moment Debra thought he would strike her. Then, with a quick movement, he jumped on Shadow and raced back down the trail.

It took a few minutes before she could do the same. The tears blinding her made it difficult to find the stirrup.

Fool, fool, fool, she raged, fighting the pain searing through her. She had soared briefly in a fool's paradise. Now his bitter denunciations told her his exact feelings.

She rode blindly, wracked by incoherent thoughts. Not until Beauty stumbled and hung a tired head did she come out of her daze.

The early mountain dusk was starting, laying deep blue shadows where golden brown had been. Marc's frequent warnings returned and she shivered, suddenly aware of the increasingly cold winds. Where was she?

She fought the cold fingers of panic threatening to

smother her. Though her world had stopped, she had no desire to be found frozen in the morning.

Think girl, think. Surely somewhere there was a recognizable landmark! She searched the area around her, then raised her eyes to the next level of mountainside.

The sinking sun glinted off something a mile or two away. Fairy Falls! She recognized the boulder clinging at the top.

With a sob of thanks she turned the horse. They had been circling in the opposite direction.

The men were in the corral saddling horses when she returned.

"Where the hell have you been!" Marc bellowed as he grabbed the reins from her cold hands.

She managed to hold on to her composure as she stared down at his angry face.

"I was just out for a ride," she said coolly. "There's no reason to be concerned. . . ."

"Concerned!" he exploded. "Concerned! I was about to send in the alarm. The boys here were all set to start searching."

Debra looked at the men. Relief was mixed with worry on their faces.

"Oh! I'm sorry, truly sorry," she apologized in a small voice.

"We wouldn't want to lose the best darned cake maker in the country," Bill said gruffly as the men dispersed.

Marc handed Beauty to Dusty. Fingers dug as a steel trap on her arms as he hurried her up the lane to the house. "Get her into a hot tub immediately," he ordered to a relieved Aunt Elsie as they entered the house.

Debra murmured words of apology as tears of weariness started down her cheeks. Was she the cause of all this turmoil?

"Hush, girl. Everything is fine now," the older woman crooned, her arm going protectively around her as she glared at her nephew.

Marc stood as in shock, seeing the tear-streaked, exhausted face. "Debra," he murmured taking a step toward her. But she was being bustled upstairs by Aunt Elsie.

It was a very subdued girl who finally descended the stairs, pink and warm from the hot tub.

"You should be in bed!" Aunt Elsie cried.

"I'm all right," Debra protested, ashamed over the distress she had caused. "I forgot how quickly the sun sets in your mountains. I was saying goodbye to my favorite places."

"Goodbye!" Aunt Elsie exclaimed. "What nonsense are you talking about?"

Debra finally had the courage to raise her eyes to look at Marc standing by the hearth.

"A wise guest doesn't overstay her welcome." Why did her voice have to quiver!

His lips compressed as a flush darkened his cheeks. Good! the shaft had gone home!

Sophia announced dinner and the uncomfortable moment passed.

"I've been very busy," Aunt Elsie said as they settled before the fire after dinner with their coffee. "I had a meeting with your brother and his contractor."

Marc stiffened, his eyes hard. "So I saw. We couldn't miss the evidence of their work today."

Aunt Elsie waved her hand airily. "Ray was just a

little ahead of himself. But it is all cleared up now. The contractor said it was feasible to move the house. The access roads would all be on the other side, as Debra suggested. You would have your ranch intact, and Ray would have his resort. Does that meet with your approval?''

There was a long, agonizing silence. Aunt Elsie's bright little eyes were fixed on Marc anxiously as he rubbed his chin in thought.

Why does he have to be so stubborn, Debra thought, *when we can all see this is the only solution?*

Finally, a wide smile broke over his stern features. "I see no objections. It is so obviously the answer that I can't believe that one of us didn't come up with it sooner!"

"That's because we didn't have Debra to help us," exclaimed Aunt Elsie. "I knew she was somebody special the first time I laid eyes on her! And I hope you realize it too, Marc Reede." She looked meaningfully at Marc before rolling up her ball of wool and sticking her knitting needles through it. "And now, children, if you'll excuse me, I think I'll go to bed."

She was alone with Marc. The realization gave her sweet pain. Yesterday, even this morning, she would have eagerly looked forward to an evening to share with him. Now she couldn't bear the hours making polite conversation.

"I think I'll go upstairs to my room," she said primly, like a little girl. "Good night, Marc."

He rose from adding a log to the fire. He looked hard at her averted face, at the defiant thrust to the jaw that contradicted the despondent droop to the lips.

"Come here, Debra," he said quietly, but it was a stern command.

She squared her shoulders as if to do battle, then let them slump back in dejection. It wasn't worth arguing about. She was too numb for anything he said to hurt anymore.

She walked slowly toward him, her eyes lowered resolutely at the carpet. She stopped a few feet from him and waited for his next words.

"I have a present," he said, nodding to the corner of the room.

Debra turned and looked in surprise at the large bundle enclosed in a plastic bag.

"Open it," he ordered. "It just arrived."

She looked wonderingly at him as she attempted to lift it. It was heavy, and she undid the plastic tie closing the opening. It felt like fur and she pulled it out, gasping as she realized what it was.

"The mountain lion!" she exclaimed. "You had the hide tanned!"

"The boys wanted to do it for you," he said, watching her face as she unrolled the soft pelt. "They worked hard to get it ready so soon."

"I hope I see them tomorrow to thank them," she said as she kneeled to spread the lovely rug on the floor. "Otherwise I will write and thank them when I get back to Denver. It will always remind me of your ranch," she said wistfully as she ran her hand over the short hair. "It will be quite the center of interest in my little apartment."

"That's funny," Marc answered. "I imagined a different place to display it."

Her head moved back in an arc as she looked up at

the tall man towering over her. The firelight flickered over his face, making it difficult to read.

"Oh?" she questioned blankly. "It wouldn't look well on one of the walls."

"I quite agree," he said blandly. "I was thinking of it by my bed."

Debra's eyes widened as her face blanched in embarrassment. She had innocently assumed the hide was for her. Hadn't he said it was a gift?

"I just haven't made up my mind if it would look best at the foot of the bed or on your side. After all, you did shoot him. It is your trophy."

Her mouth opened in amazement. Had she heard correctly?

His hands came out to capture the long fall of hair on each side of her face. He twisted his fingers in the soft folds as his palms cupped her face to raise her and pull her close. She came up hard against his muscular body. Before she could cry out, his lips came down on hers.

It was a gentle kiss, gentle and tender, and brought tears to her eyes with its very sweetness.

"Oh, Debra, girl, you'll never know the hell I went through this afternoon wondering if you were lost or perhaps hurt, and not knowing where to start looking for you," he murmured, rubbing his cheek along hers. "And it was all my fault. Don't you know I wouldn't want to live without you by my side?"

Pinwheels of excitement burst through her as the full meaning of his words unraveled along her senses. She clung helplessly in sudden weakness, leaning against the long leanness of him while waiting for him to continue.

"What's all this silly talk about leaving," he murmured as he placed light kisses along the contour of her cheek. "You don't think I'd let you escape now that I've found you. How soon can you marry me?"

She leaned back in the tight circle of his arms to look at him in astonishment.

"What?" she cried, her voice rising an octave in her bewilderment. The change was too rapid; she was being carried along in a whirlwind. Only half an hour ago she was certain tomorrow would be the last she would see him.

"I'm talking engagement," he said, his eyes crinkling in amusement over her wonder. "You, me. Followed quickly by marriage. Why did you think I wanted to give a party? I wanted to announce our engagement. That's why my initial list was so long. I wanted everyone to meet the beautiful girl I was planning to marry. Then I decided only to have my closest friends. The rest will have wait until our wedding." His face grew serious, a faint doubt clouding it. "You do want to marry me, don't you?"

She nodded wordlessly and he tightened his arms around her. "And by the way, I don't believe in long engagements. Now that I have you in my arms, I want to keep you here. As you've found out, I have a very low boiling point as far as you're concerned. After that night in my room, I had to stay away from you until you were my own dear wife. . . . Though how you could want to risk marrying me, I can't imagine. I have a vile temper, as you well know!"

Beneath his kiss Debra's lips curved into a smile.

"Oh, my darling," he groaned. "If you only knew how torn apart I was between my pride and my love for my brother. And then when you seemed to doubt me and my dreams, I exploded like an immature schoolboy." His hand went caressingly through her hair, turning her face up to his. "I've wanted you since the first day we met."

"You knew then you wanted to marry me?" she asked, stunned.

"I knew the moment you helped me down from that ledge," he confessed. "You put that cool cloth on my face. I took a good look at my charming rescuer and knew I couldn't let her escape without first trying hard to win her over to becoming a rancher's wife. You gave me a few qualms, you know," he said, sinking into an armchair and making her comfortable on his lap. His arms gripped her tightly, as if afraid even then she might escape. "But I was determined not to let you go. At least not until I had told you how much I love and need you."

Debra snuggled close to Marc and sighed in wonder. That this proud man had admitted his love for her! A beatific smile lit her face. "Oh, Marc, she whispered, "I love you. I was only waiting for you to say the words."

Marc's expression was infinitely tender as he bent to reclaim her lips. "Oh love of my life," he murmured, "sing the song of the ages with me."

Silhouette Romance

ROMANCE THE WAY IT USED TO BE... AND COULD BE AGAIN

Contemporary romances for today's women.

Each month, six very special love stories will be yours

from SILHOUETTE.

Look for them wherever books are sold

or order now from the coupon below.

$1.50 each

Silhouette Romance

___ #49 DANCER IN THE SHADOWS Wisdom	___ #60 GREEN PARADISE Hill
___ #50 DUSKY ROSE Scott	___ #61 WHISPER MY NAME Michaels
___ #51 BRIDE OF THE SUN Hunter	___ #62 STAND-IN BRIDE Halston
___ #52 MAN WITHOUT A HEART Hampson	___ #63 SNOWFLAKES IN THE SUN Brent
___ #53 CHANCE TOMORROW Browning	___ #64 SHADOW OF APOLLO Hampson
___ #54 LOUISIANA LADY Beckman	___ #65 A TOUCH OF MAGIC Hunter
___ #55 WINTER'S HEART Ladame	___ #66 PROMISES FROM THE PAST Vitek
___ #56 RISING STAR Trent	___ #67 ISLAND CONQUEST Hastings
___ #57 TO TRUST TOMORROW John	___ #68 THE MARRIAGE BARGAIN Scott
___ #58 LONG WINTER'S NIGHT Stanford	___ #69 WEST OF THE MOON St. George
___ #59 KISSED BY MOONLIGHT Vernon	

-- --

SILHOUETTE BOOKS, Department SB/1
1230 Avenue of the Americas
New York, NY 10020

Please send me the books I have checked above. I am enclosing
$_____ (please add 50¢ to cover postage and handling for each
order. NYS and NYC residents please add appropriate sales tax).
Send check or money order—no cash or C.O.D.s please. Allow six
weeks for delivery.

NAME_____

ADDRESS_____

CITY_____STATE/ZIP_____